D1539212

Sun,
Sand,
and
Sea Serpents

David Goudsward

ANOMALIST BOOKS
*San Antonio * Charlottesville*

An Original Publication of ANOMALIST BOOKS
Sun, Sand, and Sea Serpents
Copyright 2020 by David Goudsward
ISBN: 978-1-949501-11-7

On the cover: A sea monster prowls the Gulf of Mexico in a detail from the 1565 "Le Moyne Map" of Florida and Cuba, drawn in 1563 by French artist Jacques Le Moyne de Morgues and first published by Theodore de Bry in 1591.

An earlier version of Chapter 6 appeared in the *International Cryptozoology Society Journal* 1 (2017).

Book Design: Seale Studios

For information about the publisher, go to AnomalistBooks.com, or write to:
Anomalist Books, 5150 Broadway #108, San Antonio, TX 78209

Monster Diary

Other Anomalist Books by Nick Redfern

On the Trail of the Saucer Spies
There's Something in the Woods
Science Fiction Secrets
Final Events

Monster Diary

On the Road in Search of
Strange and Sinister Creatures

Nick Redfern

ANOMALIST BOOKS
San Antonio • Charlottesville

An Original Publication of ANOMALIST BOOKS

Cover image: "A Mammoth on Monument Hill" by
Daniel Eskridge

Book design by Seale Studios

For information, go to anomalistbooks.com or write to:
Anomalist Books, 5150 Broadway #108, San Antonio, TX 78209

Contents

For Paul Kimball, a good mate, and fellow paranormal road-tripper

Introduction

Monster Diary is my sixth book-length study of what have unofficially become known as cryptids—those strange, elusive entities of the woods, skies, and dark waters that have for so long fascinated countless souls all across the world. Their many memorable monikers include Sasquatch, Chupacabras, Ogopogo, Nessie, Yowie, and the Beast of Bray Road. And that's barely scratching the surface of what amounts to a vast and varied menagerie of a near-magical nature. The study of such creatures has become known as Cryptozoology.

For the mainstream cryptozoologist (some people might perceive that as being the ultimate oxymoron), the North American Bigfoot is some form of unknown ape; the creatures that inhabit the dark waters of Loch Ness, Scotland, may very well be surviving plesiosaurs; and the large and lumbering Yetis of the frozen Himalayas quite possibly represent a surviving, relic population of the mighty ape of times long-gone known as *Gigantopithecus*. And, perhaps, that is precisely what these creatures really are. I certainly don't *wholly* rule out such amazing possibilities at all. The big problem, however, is that many of the beasts that have for so long, and so diligently, been pursued are not just weird and elusive. The reality of the situation is that they are just *too* weird and *overly* elusive.

Like it or not—and, I have to say, many cryptozoologists most certainly *do not* like it, not at all, actually—there are far more than a few reports on file of Bigfoot vanishing in the blink of an eye, of cameras jamming when people try and photograph lake monsters, and of an absolute multiplicity of cryptids seen in the same location, and sometimes even during the same precise time frame as UFOs, aliens, Men in Black, spooks and specters, and other strange and unearthly phenomena. Quite clearly, normal animals cannot vanish before our very eyes, nor do they possess the ability to significantly affect the internal mechanisms of cameras, and they most assuredly should not be regularly interacting with the alleged bug-eyed denizens of far away galaxies. But the big problem for the field of cryptozoology is that this is *exactly* what these "animals" seem to be doing, time and time again, and very much more, too.

So, how does the domain of cryptozoology and its attendant

cryptozoologists deal with such rogue events? With extreme ease, the roll of an eye, and the dismissive wave of a hand, that's how. Quite often by ignoring the data and testimony, by writing the cases off as hoaxes and delusions, or suggesting that while the witnesses were certainly earnest and honest, they just *had* to have been mistaken in their interpretation of what occurred. Case closed. Well, no, case *not* closed actually. I have never understood the zeal (sometimes even the outright and outrageous hostile zeal) that accompanies the point of view that the cryptids of our world *must* be flesh and blood creatures, and absolutely nothing else, come the proverbial hell or high water.

Because I simply don't understand that rigid approach, I have never felt any need or desire to adhere to it in the slightest. Instead, I do precisely what I have always done. That is, I carefully follow the trail, the evidence, and the witness testimony and see where it all leads. Then, having done so, I try and make some sense of it and attempt to reach some kind of conclusion, regardless of which avenue that approach ultimately led me to, even if it's one I didn't previously consider viable.

And that's what you will find within the pages of *Monster Diary*: A study of strange tales of savage beasts that paradoxically seem as real as they do unreal, and of bizarre life-forms that clearly, and obviously, challenge the accepted wisdom of both cryptozoology and science. But none of that negates an important, overriding fact that must be stressed from the very outset: Our marauding monsters of the woods, waters, and skies most certainly *do* exist. But, many of them, I personally conclude, are not what they seem to be at first glance, or what cryptozoology wishes, wants, or prefers them to be. Read on, and, I sincerely hope, you'll come to see exactly why.

Nick Redfern
Arlington, Texas
August 2012

Chapter 1
Creatures of the Phantom Kind

"Seeing it was scary, but a privilege, too."

Extinction vs. Existence

The mammoth was a majestic creature that roamed the lonely wilds of North America, the vast expanses of Western Europe, and the harsh, frozen lands of northern Russia during the Pleistocene era. It is generally accepted as having finally become extinct at some time around the end of the last Ice Age. Today, all we have left of this huge, mighty beast are a number of fairly well preserved carcasses found embedded in icy tombs, and the various bone and tusk fragments that still continue to surface from time to time. Could there, however, still possibly be more—maybe even *much* more— just waiting to be uncovered? That, incredibly, was precisely the controversial claim made to me as the year 2009 began. [1]

For centuries intriguing and admittedly sensational rumors have surfaced to the effect that in some of the more remote parts of our planet the mammoth just might still exist, blissfully unaware of what such a shocking and jaw-dropping revelation would mean to the world's zoological community, if one day fully confirmed. And while such a scenario is certainly controversial in the extreme, and one that is completely derided by mainstream science and zoology, perhaps it is not entirely out of the question.

For example, the related dwarf mammoths of Wrangel Island, which is located in the Arctic Ocean, are known to have lived until approximately 1,700 to 1,500 BC, which is itself rather startling. [2] But far more controversial are those claims suggesting that the mammoth still walks the frozen tundra and forests of the north to this very day. "Absolute nonsense!" some might say. And if we're brutally honest with ourselves, almost everyone would probably say that such a thing is nonsense. A few, however, are inclined to argue strongly with that assertion, and maybe with very good reason, if their astonishing, collective tales can be believed.

In the late 19th century, a researcher and adventurer named Bengt

Sjogren heard tales of the giant, hairy, tusked creatures that lived in the huge, ancient forests in the remote parts of Alaska. The reports of these "hairy elephants"—as they were described in the stories told to Sjogren— extended to equally wild and remote parts of both Canada and Siberia. [3]

Similarly, in February 1888, the New Zealand-based *Argus* newspaper reported on the apparent discovery in Alaska of strange, large tracks that had been found by the Stick Indians in the vicinity of the winding White River. At the time of the discovery, the excited *Argus* journalist wrote: "One of the Indians said that while hunting, he came across an immense track sunk several inches in the moss and larger around than a barrel. The Indian followed up the curious trail, and at last came in full view of his game. These Indians as a class are the bravest of hunters, but the immense proportions of this new kind of game filled the hunter with fear, and he took to swift and immediate flight. He described it as being larger than the post trader's store, with great shining, yellowish tusks, and a mouth large enough to swallow him at a single gulp." [4]

Then, during October 1899, the highly controversial story surfaced of one Henry Tukeman, a man who claimed to have killed a mammoth, the remains of which were said to have been subsequently donated to the Smithsonian Institute in Washington, D.C. The tale was loudly denounced as nothing more than a sensationalized hoax, or a tale that weaved fact and fiction in blurry, Gonzo-style fashion, which is what it may very well have been. Even today, however, some mammoth researchers still cling to the tenuous belief and hope that Tukeman's tale just might have had far more than a grain of truth to it, and that the hoax angle was possibly introduced to try and lay to rest a controversy that no-one within mainstream science wished to deal with or confront. [5] And also in the late 1800s, several reports of what were termed "large, shaggy beasts" were given to Russian authorities by Siberian tribesman, but no proof was ever forthcoming. [6]

The sensational stories don't end there, however.

French charge d'affaire, M. Gallon, was working in Vladivostok in 1946, and revealed that, more than 25 years earlier, he had met with a Russian fur-trapper who claimed to have seen living "giant, furry elephants" residing deep inside the taiga. Gallon added that the trapper appeared to have no previous knowledge of mammoths and seemingly had no visible reason to make up such a wild and unbelievable story. [7] A further sighting allegedly occurred during the Second World War when a Soviet Air Force pilot reported seeing a small herd of such creatures while flying over the frozen wastelands of Siberia. [8]

So does the legendary Mammoth of times past really still exist, utterly flying in the face of accepted wisdom? Or are all of the amazing tales merely friend-of-a-friend accounts, myths, hoaxes, and misidentifications? Personally, I have been fascinated—perhaps even slightly obsessed—by these engaging and outrageous stories for years. And, just like *The X-Files'* famous motto "I want to believe," I really do. The skeptical and logical parts of my brain, however, tells me that the mammoth is an utterly dead creature, one whose existence came to a tragic and definitive end thousands of years ago, other than in the movies, of course. (There's the *Mammoth* movie of 2006, British TV's *Primeval,* and the 2008 Hollywood production *10,000 BC.*) [9]

But who can deny the appeal that these stories create in the minds of thrill-seekers just about everywhere? I certainly can't, that's for sure. If there was one expedition I could go on, and if both funding and time were utterly unlimited, it would be to the old stomping grounds of the mammoth. Okay, I know full well that the chances of actually finding a living, breathing mammoth are not just miniscule, they're *beyond* miniscule. But as long as there is even the very remotest of all possibilities, I know I'll never be truly satisfied until I go and seek out the creature for myself. Until, or unless, that day hopefully comes, however, I can only continue to wonder if, far from prying eyes, small pockets of mammoth continue to walk the earth. But we're not quite done yet with the mighty marauding beast of times long gone.

A Mammoth of the Mysterious Kind

There is yet another aspect to this controversial story, and it's one that's downright spooky, too. It came to me on January 2, 2009, from a woman named Jill O'Brien, and it is still to this day one of the oddest tales to have ever crossed my path. And believe me: my path has crossed with many a weird tale!

On September 18, 2008, Jill claims to have come face to face with a baby mammoth in Alaska's Wrangell-St. Elias National Park and Preserve. Well, this was a case I certainly could not afford to ignore, especially since Jill at the time was living in Oklahoma City, which was only a few hours' drive from my home in Arlington, Texas. That's right: road-trip. And so, I elected to zoom northwards in search of perhaps one of the very few people to claim a sighting of a still-living mammoth. But as will shortly become clear, things weren't quite so...well...clear!

I hit the road very early on a torturously cold morning, and by lunchtime I was sitting opposite Jill, in the small, rented apartment that was her home before she moved to Lincoln, Nebraska, in late February. The skeptics and naysayers just love to try and portray those who claim encounters of the truly unusual kind to be slightly off-kilter (or worse); but no such thing could be said about Jill. Very down to earth, lucid and intelligent, she worked for a well-known, now defunct bookstore chain, and related her remarkable story to me in a fashion that was refreshingly coherent and clear.

Established in 1980 by the Alaska National Interest Lands Conservation Act, Wrangell-St. Elias National Park can officially boast of being the largest U.S. National Park, covering no less than 20,587 square-miles, which, trivia fans may possibly be interested to know, is greater than the land mass of nine of the 50 American states. It was very near to the base of the 18,009-foot-tall Mount St. Elias, which can be found in the park and which borders the Yukon-Alaskan border, that Jill's uncanny encounter took place. [10]

Jill told me that she had a particular passion for photographing mountains, and Mount St. Elias was one that she wished to preserve for posterity in her ever growing collection of picture albums. She was all set up to take a "great shot" of the mountain, when to her left she heard "a funny crunching and thudding on the ground." Jill turned her head to see where the sound was coming from and was "totally freaked" to see a small mammoth, "maybe four feet [in height]," race past her, glance quickly in her direction as it did so, and then vanish into what resembled a "small, black cloud of smoke that sucked into itself and was gone."

Jill fully conceded that the event, which lasted perhaps no more than six or seven seconds, stretched credulity to its absolute limit. But as she told me in tones that came across as being wholly earnest in nature: "It was a mammoth, it was a baby mammoth. It was there one second, then it looked at me, and it was gone, like it went invisible or just vanished. But that *is* what happened. Sorry, I know it's probably not going to interest you." Needless to say, it most assuredly *did* interest me, for reasons that will soon become clear. [11]

The Saber-Toothed Specter

Jill O'Brien's story eerily paralleled the story told me by Jenny Burrows, who also contacted me in January 2009, and who had a creepy tale to tell of a creature she claimed to have encountered only days before in a particularly dense area of Seattle woodland. A week or so after speaking with Jenny on the telephone, I had the chance to interview her in person, as luck or fate would have it, after I was interviewed at the base of Mount Rainier, Washington, for a British TV production on UFOs and the famous Kenneth Arnold sighting of June 24, 1947. With the show wrapped up, I checked into a motel for the night, then the following morning grabbed a rental car and made my way to Seattle to speak to Jenny.

Jenny's story was undeniably freaky. Her encounter, she assured me, involved a fully-grown Smilodon, which is more popularly known as a saber-tooth tiger. Yes, you read that right. But, the kicker was that Jenny's saber-tooth tiger was apparently spectral in nature, very much like Jill O'Brien's baby Mammoth. The saber-tooth tiger, a massive, muscular killing machine that weighed up to 900 pounds and which roamed and prowled both North and South America as far back as 2.5 Million B.C., is widely assumed to have become extinct around 10,000 years ago. No one anywhere on the surface of this planet should be seeing such a beast today. But Jenny Burrows most certainly begs to differ. [12]

In the world of on-screen fantasy, this marauding and ferocious predator is a regular player, and one for whom extinction plays absolutely no role at all. There was the movie, *Sabretooth*, that made its debut on the SyFy Channel in November 2002, and in which a scientist uses fossilized DNA to bring such a beast back to life. Unsurprisingly, the animal goes on a murderous spree, slaughtering pretty much all of the cast of the movie one by one. [13] In addition, in an episode of Britain's hit TV show *Primeval*, a character named Valerie finds a saber-tooth tiger cub that has stumbled through a time portal to present day England. And, you may ask, what does Valerie do? Well, the first thing she does is to hide the creature in her garage. That is, at least, until it grows at an alarming rate, inevitably escapes, and causes chaos, death and disaster at a local amusement park. [14]

So much for televised fantasy, but what of the real world? Could it really be the case that the saber-tooth tiger still exists, hiding out from one and all in the many thick woods and forests of the United States, and maybe elsewhere also? When the bare bones of Jenny's story were initially related to me a week or so earlier, I figured that this was the angle she was trying to promote. But as she told her story, it became very apparent that her tale was far stranger than that – and much more intriguing, too, I now have to confess.

According to Jenny, she had been walking through the dense woods with her pet Labrador dog, Bobbie, when it suddenly stopped in its tracks, whined loudly, and dropped to the floor, shaking almost uncontrollably. Thinking that her faithful pet had possibly had a seizure of some sort, Jenny quickly bent down to comfort the dog and saw that it was staring intently to its left. Following Bobbie's terrified gaze, Jenny was horrified to see moving in clandestine fashion in the undergrowth what looked like a large cat, "like a mountain lion, but it was much bigger." That the creature was possibly a mountain lion quite understandably filled Jenny's mind with dread, dread which was amplified to stratospheric proportions when its face could clearly be seen, including the two huge teeth that were the absolute hallmarks of the saber-tooth tiger. As Jenny said to me, and with much justification: "You don't have to work in a zoo or [be] an archaeologist to know what a saber-tooth looks like: *everyone* knows."

It was then, however, that Jenny's story became even more bizarre, and chillingly and closely echoed that of Jill O'Brien. As the saber-toothed monster loomed fully into view and out of the confines of the bushes and undergrowth, Jenny could see that its body seemed to be semi-transparent. "The bottom of its front paws were missing or invisible," she told me. "It looked at me with a sort of surprise when it saw me watching it, and it knew I had seen it, and then it was gone, just like that. It was terrifying, absolutely terrifying, but it was a beautiful animal, too. Seeing it was scary, but a privilege, too."

Jenny concluded that what she was had encountered in the woods was not a still-living saber-tooth tiger at all. Rather, she thought it "had to be the ghost of a saber-tooth" that was still faithfully haunting its old pathways and ancient hunting grounds, thousands of years after its physical death. Assuming Jenny had related her story accurately and without exaggeration, it was nigh-on impossible for me to disagree with her conclusion. [15]

Phantom Apes and Monkeys

One month or so after I spoke with Jill O'Brien and Jenny Burrows, there was yet another development in my quest for the truth about spectral animals. For years, I have had a deep fascination with a particular so-called British Bigfoot. It is said to haunt the tree-shrouded areas of England's Shropshire Union Canal, specifically in and around the old village of Ranton, Staffordshire. So fascinated am I by the damned critter, I even wrote a book about it: *Man-Monkey*. [16]

This story has its origins in 1879, when a man walking home late at night, with his horse and cart in-tow, claimed to have been attacked by a bizarre ape-man-like beast while crossing Bridge 39 on the canal. Hairy, fast-moving, and possessed of a pair of self-illuminating white eyes, it ultimately vanished into the night. And according to the testimony of the witness, the beast was distinctly spectral in nature. The man said that as he struck the beast with his horse-whip, the whip actually passed right through the creature's hairy body. Sightings of the Man-Monkey have abounded in the area ever since. My current count of cases is now upwards of 30, covering the period from the late 1800s and right up until 2007.

In February 2009, a fascinating new development in the strange saga surfaced, and maybe, just maybe, it opened some doors to the question of what the Man-Monkey really was, is, or may have been. The story came from an historian named Mike Dash. As Dash said at the time, he had then recently been leafing through a copy of the December 8, 1878, edition of *Sheldrake's Aldershot & Sandhurst Military Gazette*, and had come across an amazing story in its pages:

"CAPTURING A GORILLA IN SHROPSHIRE: For a fortnight past the district around Madely Wood, Salop, has been in a state of intense excitement, by the alleged depredations committed by a gorilla, which is said to have escaped from a wild beast menagerie travelling to Bridgnorth. The animal was stated to have first made his appearance in the neighbourhood of that town, where in the darkness of the night it was severally seen by a clergyman and a policeman, both of whom fled.

"It is also said to have appeared at several places in the immediate neighbourhood. A few evenings since the occupier of a house in Madely Wood went to bed at a reasonable hour, with the greater portion of his family, leaving his 'gude wife' up, who took the opportunity to visit a neighbour, leaving the door open and a candle burning.

"Returning in a short time, she was horrified at seeing a bent form, with a goodly array of gray hair around its face, crouching over the expiring embers of the fire, apparently warming itself, the light having gone out. Too frightened to shriek, she ran to her neighbours, who quickly armed themselves with pokers, iron bars, guns, and pitchforks and other instruments of a similar character, and marched in a body to capture the gorilla.

"The form was seen sitting at the fire, but evidently aroused by the approaching body, rose to its full height and revealed the figure of an eccentric character well known in the neighbourhood as 'Old Johnny,' who seeing the door open had quietly walked in to light his pipe, accidentally 'puffed' the candle out, and was very near being captured, if not exterminated, in mistake for an escaped gorilla.

"The animal has not been heard of since." [17]

I found this quite fascinating as the story had surfaced only one month before the Man-Monkey was seen on the Shropshire Union Canal and in the very same English county of Shropshire, no less. And as Mike Dash astutely noted: "Old Johnny and his humorous encounter make for an interesting story, and it's easy to see why the journalist who wrote the piece focused on him. As published, though, the article ignores the central question of what became of Shropshire's mysterious 'gorilla'. The wild-beast-escaped-from-a-travelling menagerie is a common motif in out of place animal stories...But it would be an ambitious showman who kept an animal as dangerous as a gorilla in a travelling show." [18]

I knew that Mike Dash was absolutely right. Numerous stories, tales and rumors of circus escapees (in Britain, the U.S., and just about everywhere) have been dutifully trotted out time and again to account for sightings of exotic animals in areas where they have absolutely no business roaming. A perfect case in point: Britain's big cats. In his classic title of 1986, *Cat Flaps*, British Fortean author Andy Roberts discussed a wave of big cat sightings in the English county of Yorkshire during the 1980s. One particular series of encounters led a certain commentator on the affair to quietly confide in Andy: "They all come from Knaresborough Zoo, you know." [19]

There was no evidence at all that the now closed down Knaresborough Zoo, situated in Harrogate, Yorkshire, had lost any big cats, yet such tales and theories often spring up in such situations. Is that what happened back in 1878? Had someone, or as the *Gazette's* story suggests, several people, seen a weird Bigfoot-like entity that was subsequently explained away (but without any actual evidence to support the notion), as having escaped from a travelling menagerie? Or, incredibly, was the story actually true? Could there really have been a roaming circus from which a fully grown gorilla made a successful bid for freedom? And if so, did it ultimately find its way, one dark and winter's night in January 1879, to the Shropshire Union Canal, where it almost scared the life out of the man who had the misfortune to encounter it while crossing over Bridge 39? Maybe, but that that would certainly not explain the seemingly spectral nature of the beast reported at the canal, nor would it explain how sightings of the same beast have continued until pretty much the present day. Unless, that is, what people are seeing today could be the ghostly form of a long dead gorilla, one that is forever doomed to haunt and wander the tree-shrouded, old canal, rather like Jill O'Brien's mammoth at Alaska's Wrangell-St. Elias National Park and Preserve, and Jenny Burrows' Smilodon in Seattle.

A Ghost-Hunter Speaks

Can it be true? Are ghostly big cats *really* roaming the woods of the Pacific Northwest? Are the wilds of Alaska home to genuine, spectral mammoths? And does a phantom ape, or gorilla, continue to make its home in the woods that surround a particular stretch of old English canal? Perhaps the idea is not quite as outlandish as it might appear at first glance. When we chatted in 2010 about such specific and controversial matters, paranormal expert and good friend Joshua P. Warren, the author of *Pet Ghosts*, told me that he had extensively investigated a series of encounters with apparitional ancient animals on farmland at Lancaster, South Carolina, one of which seemed to resemble a ghostly pterodactyl. Josh told me he had mused deeply upon the possibility that the paranormal presence of certain extinct animals might very well help explain at least *some* sightings of monstrous beasts in our presence to this very day, and particularly so those that seemingly appear and vanish in the blink of the proverbial eye.

"Maybe Bigfoot is a phantimal," said Josh to me, utilizing a term he uses to describe ghostly beasts, "perhaps even the ghost of a prehistoric creature, similar to the enormous extinct possible ape, *Gigantopithecus*, or maybe even the spirits of primitive humans." And, in a similar fashion, Josh explained to me, he was not adverse to the idea that the world's most famous lake-monster, Nessie, might actually represent some form of "ghostly plesiosaur," rather than a literal, living animal or even a colony of animals. [20]

This latter point was closely echoed by investigative author Jim Marrs, another good friend of mine, who lives just a short drive from where I live. While digging deep into the subject of the U.S. Government's secret research into the realms of so-called remote viewing and psychic spying, Jim learned that elements of the official world had secretly attempted to focus their skills upon solving the riddle of what it is that lurks within the waters of Loch Ness, Scotland. It was a very controversial operation, and it led, Jim noted, to an amazing conclusion.

"Several sessions targeting the famous Loch Ness monster," said Jim, "revealed physical traces of the beast—a wake in the water, movement of a large body underwater. Their drawings even resembled a prehistoric plesiosaur, often identified as matching descriptions of Nessie. But when the viewers tried to discover where the object came from or returned to, they hit a dead end. The creature seemed to simply appear and disappear. Considering that reports of human ghosts date back throughout man's history, the Psi Spies seriously considered the possibility that the Loch Ness monster is nothing less than a dinosaur's ghost." [21]

Do the spirits of long-extinct animals still roam the Earth? Could such a theory account for both Jill O'Brien's sighting of a mammoth in the woods of Alaska, and Jenny Burrows' encounter with a saber-tooth tiger outside of Seattle? It was certainly an intriguing idea, I thought, one that might very well go some way towards explaining how, and why, supposedly extinct creatures that surface from time to time always seem to remain so bafflingly elusive and carefully avoid all attempts to capture or kill them. Whatever the ultimate truth of the matter, it was certainly a most curious and captivating way for me to start a new year of monstrous investigations.

Chapter 2
Beware the Beast of Bodalog

"The life of a creature is in the blood."

The Rise of the Sheep Slaughterer

One thing that never ceases to amaze me with respect to monster hunting is that to try and uncover some startling truths about these strange and terrible creatures, it's not always necessary to embark upon lengthy voyages to far-away lands. Sometimes you only need to hang around in your very own stomping grounds to stumble on something truly abominable.

The oldest town in mid Wales, and one with an abundance of cairns and old standing-stones at the foot of which the ancients dutifully worshipped, Rhayader is a definitively atmospheric locale. It's one very much filled with rich history and magical folklore. For example, 5,000-year-old Neolithic axes are periodically discovered there, and in 1899 a collection of gold jewelry was unearthed on nearby Gwastedyn Hill that was thought to have originated with a 5th century princess named Rowena, the daughter of an Anglo-Saxon leader, Hengest, and wife to High King Vortigern, who was a powerful and brutal warlord in his own right. [1]

Against this notable and historic backdrop, between the months of September and December 1988, a series of very unusual animal killings occurred in and around the vicinity of Rhayader that had the people of the area in absolute fits of frenzy and fear. Without doubt, the Bodalog Farm, which was owned by the Pugh family, suffered most horrifically of all. No less than 35 sheep were violently mutilated and slaughtered in that time-frame by a stealthy unknown predator whose modus operandi was always exactly the same: a deep and fatal bite to the sternum, almost exclusively delivered when darkness had fallen all across the area.

When the actions of the foul beast began to take an increasing toll upon both farm animals and local livelihood, foxhounds were dispatched and the scent of the mysterious killer was picked up on several occasions. Yet each and every time, the creature utterly and skillfully eluded the pursuing dogs. Although both the local and national press made very big and exciting waves about a marauding and savage "black panther" being on the loose, in reality something much stranger was afoot. On no occasion was any kind of telltale paw-print ever found that might have led one to assume that a large cat of some type was indeed roaming the fringes and farms of the town, as the media loudly and sensationally suggested might be the case.

Instead, those farmers whose sheep had been fatally savaged discovered certain areas of field and grassland that had been laid totally flat by whatever had been circling and stalking the sheep before moving in for the kill—something that, quite justifiably, suggested the presence of an incredibly long, huge, heavy, slithering snake. This particular theory was given still more credence locally when yet more areas of flattened grass were uncovered that led to the nearby River Wye, which, at an impressive 134 miles in length, is the fifth longest river in the United Kingdom.

Many of the worried farmers who had worked the local land for years, and in some cases for decades, concluded that something monstrous and unspeakable was surfacing from the dark waters late at night, making its careful way to the fields, and then mutilating the sundry animal population of Rhayader with truly frightening speed and cold and calculated precision. There was even whispered talk of those animals being drained of huge quantities of blood, stories that were not entirely denied by the puzzled and slightly embarrassed local police. No wonder, then, that the townsfolk were keeping their doors and windows firmly locked at night—and sometimes during daylight hours, too. [2]

The giant-snake theory was certainly an ingenious and imaginative one, but as my good mate, Richard Freeman, of the Center for Fortean Zoology correctly noted, it was a highly problematic and dubious theory, too. "Britain's only venomous snake, the adder *Vipera berus*, is far too small to have killed all these sheep," noted Richard. "This case begs many odd questions: why would an animal go to all the trouble of wasting venom and energy killing so many sheep, then not eat any? If it was a large, exotic, venomous snake that had escaped from captivity, how did it cope with October in Wales?" [3]

A former zoo-keeper who specialized in reptiles, Richard was absolutely right: the cold and harsh Welsh weather at that time of year would have rendered any large snake practically immobile, if not even killed it very quickly indeed. Nevertheless, the mystery continued at a frightful pace, until two months later, when the terrible slaughter stopped abruptly, much to the relief of the population of Rhayader. And, with no firm answer to the mystery, the local police quietly closed its strange dossier on the matter, the media moved on to pastures and stories new, and the residents of Rhayader tried to forget about the traumatic, terror-driven past few months. Dark memories aside, that would very likely have been the end of the matter had it not been for the fact that the Beast of Bodalog briefly returned to its old haunts in the summer of 2009 (very curiously at the same time that astonishing data on *other* slithering, coiling British monsters surfaced, as I will relate in the next chapter).

A Nightmare Returns to Rhayader

The new story came to me from a man named Huw Fowler, an artist, fisherman, and blacksmith who claimed to have seen the vile monster negotiating the old waters of the River Wye late in June 2009, and who emailed me a few weeks later with the details. Fowler searched the internet and found an article on my *There's Something in the Woods* blog about some 1980s sightings of giant eels in the British Isles. This blog post prompted him to contact me. [4] More importantly, Fowler offered to show me the precise location where the amazing new encounter occurred, and share the full details of the story, the next time I was back in Britain. As luck would have it, in August 2009 I was scheduled to speak at two England-based, paranormal-themed events: the Weird Weekend and Weird '09, the latter in the historic, UFO-saturated town of Warminster. So, with a couple of weeks' time available to me, I vowed to dig as deeply as possible into the tale of Huw Fowler. To do so meant there was only one option available to me: I needed to head out to the sinister scene myself and do a bit of detective work.

On a Wednesday morning in August, I flew from Dallas-Fort Worth International Airport to London, hung out at my dad's place for two nights, and the next day– fully recovered from jet-lag— hit the road to Rhayader on a Friday night, thus ensuring that it would be nearing the witching-hour when I finally arrived. I figured I would park somewhere near to where both the old and the new action occurred, and see if my quarry, under cover of the pitch-black darkness that enveloped the rural area after the sun had set, just might surface. Given the sinister circumstances, I surmised, midnight would be a highly appropriate time to make my arrival.

"Don't let some monster wreck my bloody car!" bellowed my dad, in concerned and grumbling tones, as I pulled out of the driveway in his compact white Fiat.

"I'll try not to!" I shouted out of the window, as I spun the tires and zoomed off into the dark, silent, foggy night, while *Oasis* boomed out of the car's speakers. I was on my way, in search of a blood-drinking monster that roamed the wild fields and winding waters of Wales. Sadly, despite my night-long stake-out at the water's edge, that saw me equipped with flashlight and audio-visual recording equipment, my quarry did not surface from the bitterly cold darkness of the River Wye. With two full days at my disposal, however, I was not about to give up the chase that easily, in fact, I did not give up at all. The best place to go to catch the gossip on all matters mysterious are, of course, the local pubs. And there were plenty of them in that little Welsh town. Rhayader actually has the wonderful and highly enviable distinction of having the most pubs per capita in the entire United Kingdom; the town can currently boast of one pub for approximately every 170 people. I seriously thought about moving there for a while. My first stop was the old Crown Inn on North Street, which was near the bursting point that Saturday night.

Even though this new story, rather curiously, did not apparently reach the eyes and ears of the local media, one of the drinkers told me "the press have been silenced," which I considered to be an extremely doubtful and pretty much fanciful assertion. There was certainly a degree of hushed talk in the pub concerning "the beast" and its monstrous predations. It was, without doubt, just like late 1988 again, albeit significantly scaled down in terms of coverage and hysteria. Monster-talk was the order of the day, even if this time it seemed the locals were determined to keep things about as low-key as possible. This was actually not a particularly difficult task to achieve, since Rhayader is a small, very close-knit community with a population of just slightly above 2,000. Plus, this time—unlike in 1988, when incidents were occurring all around the area, thus making it impossible to keep things under wraps—there was only one report: that of Huw Fowler. I decided the wisest approach was to keep my eyes and ears open, mingle amongst the merry throng, and basically listen it on their conversations whenever and wherever possible.

There were a couple of folks who were insisting a "new big cat" had chosen Rhayader as its latest hunting-ground. And there was one who spoke of exotic pets, such as pythons and boa constrictors. There was even the story—the very bizarre story, it must be said—suggesting that a Komodo Dragon had escaped from a private enclosure and was now wildly feeding upon just about anything and everything that dared to cross its path. That there was no evidence of anyone in the area having ever owned a Komodo Dragon, never mind having disastrously misplaced one, seemed not to matter to those who were in on the conversation. Far more intriguing to me was the theory being discussed, by a group of five or six, that a gang of occultists in the area had "conjured up" the killer-beast, and that, incredibly, it was being deliberately provided with a welcome supply of sheep as a form of ancient, sacrificial appeasement. Now *that* was much more like it!

I decided to make my move and approached the group. I explained what I was doing in town, told them of my deep interest in the original animal mutilation affair of 21 years previously, and asked if I might join them for a genial chat about slithering monsters, flattened grass, and sheep of the dead and mutilated variety. They looked at me, went noticeably quiet for a moment or two, and then whispered and scowled amongst themselves – rather in the fashion of some shadowy group guarding some equally shadowy conspiracy of a scale that would have even eclipsed the Roswell event of 1947 and the JFK assassination of 1963 combined. But when I offered to buy the next two rounds of beer for each of them, suddenly the dark atmosphere changed, and it was all jollity, handshakes, and smiles. And so it was that a truly unsettling story unfolded before my eyes and ears.

Faust Would be Proud

"Never you mind what the newspapers said in 1988," one old, gnarly farmer said to me in knowing tones, as he tapped the top of the table with his cigarette-stained index finger. He assured me that the stories of big cats and snakes on the loose, both back then and now, were all complete and utter "bollocks." Rather, he explained, while the rest of the group huddled ever closer and listened carefully, it was a fact that Rhayader had a small band of occultists in its midst who had been employing archaic rite and ritual as means to summon up a supernatural beast known as a Kelpie.

According to ancient Scottish legend, the Kelpie or water-horse, as it is also called, is a paranormal creature that haunts rivers, pools, and lakes, and has the uncanny ability to alter its appearance, to shape-shift, in other words. The most common form the Kelpie adopts is that of a horse, hence the name applied to it, the water-horse. It stands by the water's edge, tempting any passing and weary traveler who might consider continuing on his or her journey to mount it. That, however, is always the fatal downfall of the traveler, as invariably the beast then rears violently and charges head-long into the depths of the waters, thus drowning its terrified rider in the process. The Kelpie is also said to be able to transform itself into both a beautiful maiden, or mermaid, and a large, hairy man not unlike Bigfoot, interestingly, that typically hides in the vegetation of both natural and man-made waterways and leaps out and attacks the unwary. Actually, that's not at all unlike the actions of the Man-Monkey, of the Shropshire Union Canal, back in 1879. Fair enough, I opined, but why on earth would someone want to deliberately bring into our world such a horrific entity from whatever dark domain it called home? [5]

The answer, so I was told, was actually very simple, but steeped in swirling controversy: appeasing the Kelpie with a tasty sacrificial animal or several is all but guaranteed to provide the conjurer, or the conjurers, with good health, much wealth, and great power and influence. It was, undeniably, a typical Faustian pact. The problem, I was told, was that "the creature has got out of control," and as a consequence had now returned to our plane of existence from the diabolical realm to which it had vanished back in the latter days of 1988. Like some unruly, spoiled and monstrous teenage brat, it was now demanding more and more sustenance from those who had dared call it forth. That sustenance was in the form of the blood of the unfortunate farm animals that it encountered during the course of its late night excursions. Hardly surprising, I thought. After all, when does a Faustian pact ever have even a remotely positive outcome? Never!

One informed old soul, who was deep in on the conversation from the very beginning, asked me, while sporting a menacing glare: "Do you know your *Leviticus*?" I confessed that, no, I did not know my *Leviticus*. He then quietly and concisely quoted to me from *17:11*: "The life of a creature is in the blood." [6]

My original informant sat back, sipped on his pint of bitter, and allowed his equally aged and conspiratorial friend to take the reins of the rest of the story, which was a brief yet illuminating one. It basically went something like this: blood, as a definitive life-force, contains certain qualities that border upon the paranormal, and if one knows the ancient, sacrificial ways of the "old-ones" (yes, I know, definitive shades of H.P. Lovecraft), it can be used to feed, nourish and appease terrible entities from the twilight dimensions.

"In return for the blood, the person who has called them in gets their reward: money, whatever," one of the shadowy group told me. As an author always short of cash, I considered making a joke, asking when and where I could sign up, but ultimately thought better of it. When I inquired how, precisely, they knew all this, a hushed tone descended upon one and all, and I learned no more—not from that curious band, anyway. So after a couple more pints of fine ale, I bid them all farewell, they duly did likewise, and I stepped out of the Crown Inn and into the cold, bleak night. By now the rest of the pubs were also on the verge of closing their old doors too, and so the chances of learning more that night were slim, I realized.

As I carefully scanned the dark shadows of the town, I felt like I had been inserted into the pages of some vile and stinking saga worthy of H.P. Lovecraft himself. If I had, this one appeared to be all too real. I slept on the back seat of the car that night, curled up under a couple of blankets I had the foresight to bring with me, at the edge of a desolate, windswept field overlooking the cursed locale. Then, the following day, I drove to my next port of call, the home of the man who was responsible for getting me into this monstrous mess in the first place, Huw Fowler.

As I made my way to Fowler's abode the next morning, I mused upon the words of the shadowy group in the Crown Inn the previous night. Was some sort of unholy sacrifice *really* afoot in the area? As fantastic as such a scenario might have sounded to me at the time, I knew it could not be ruled out entirely. Up and down the entire length and breadth of the River Wye, there were longstanding beliefs and old traditions about how the river gods of ancient times could supposedly be appeased with a once a year sacrifice of the human variety. So, that much of the story, if nothing else, could certainly be verified.

As prime evidence of this, in 1912 Ella Leather wrote in the pages of *The Folk-Lore of Herefordshire* that in the latter part of the 19th century, a young boy from the nearby town of Ross drowned in the River Wye. The boy's tragic death, it was accepted by many superstitious locals, ensured that all of the remaining children in the area would have nothing to fear by swimming in the river, not for another full year, anyway. "The river has had its due," were the chilling words of one resident of Ross, as detailed in the pages of Leather's old book. I scanned the depressing, cloud-filled skyline, and as I got closer to Fowler's abode, pondered and brooded on the sacrificial side of the stories related by Ella Leather back in 1912, and to me almost a full century later. [7]

A New Witness Speaks

Huw Fowler lived in an old stone cottage situated approximately a 40-minute drive from Rhayader. The cottage looked like it would have been very much at home within the pages of some old novel befitting the likes of the Bronte sisters, Sir Arthur Conan Doyle, or M.R. James. And having greeted me at the doorstep, the 60-something Fowler warmly invited me in and provided me with a welcome bowl of hot, thick potato soup and a chilled pint of lager. This was not at all a bad way to get quickly refueled on a lunchtime Saturday in mid Wales, I thought. As I tucked into my meal and drink, Fowler told me how, on the night that his life was forever changed, he was fishing on the banks of the River Wye, when suddenly he spotted a large, black, glossy-looking beast moving slowly and—rather surprisingly given that it was at least 15 feet in length—near silently through the cold moonlit waters.

The best way that Fowler could describe the animal was as "a big worm or eel." He added: "It had a sort of wormy, eely movement, and there was a small head, like a seal's—tiny, actually—which was sat on its neck, about two-feet up out of the water, and it moved around like it was looking for something. It was almost like it was nosey."

"What did you do?" I asked.

He laughed, shrugged his shoulders, and shook his head in an exasperated fashion: "Well, I watched it, didn't I? I just sat there. It didn't hang around or nothing. It was like it knew where it was going. It was like it was on a mission, or something. The body, what I could see, was about a foot [in thickness], and I know there's not supposed to be anything like that in these parts."

"Or in *any* parts," I added.

Fowler agreed, and continued: "I told some of my fishing mates in Rhayader, and then it got out around town a bit." I nodded and informed Fowler that the affair had been widely, if very quietly, discussed the previous night in the *Crown Inn*. "I know," he replied, with a slight grimace on his face and a sigh in his voice. "It's alright, though. I *do* want to know what it was."

"You know what they're saying in Rhayader, don't you?" I asked.

"That it's all to do with devil-worship, or something like that?" Fowler responded. I nodded again, and he added: "Well, I don't know about all that, but I did see *something*." [8]

Of that, there seemed, to me, very little doubt. To his credit, Fowler did not try to elaborate on his tale of wormy terror. Instead, he merely repeated the scant but fascinating facts again, and I ended up hanging out with him until the early hours of the following morning, discussing Welsh folklore, wizardry, and mythology, before driving back to my dad's place, and returning his prized Fiat, which was fortunately unscathed by marauding monsters of the murky waters of Wales.

I still keep in touch with Fowler to this day, and we have even developed a good friendship (in 2010, he came to stay with me in Texas for four days, while on a two-week vacation in the U.S.). But the worm, the eel, the Beast of Bodalog, the conjured nightmare, or whatever it really was, has not surfaced again. Unless, you know something that I, Huw Fowler, and the conspiratorial crowd at *the Crown Inn* don't.

Chapter 3
The Great Eel Hunt

"It's like something out of a horror movie."

There's something in the Water

My brief trip to Rhayader was now behind me, but my quest to seek out the coiling, water-based monstrosities of Britain most certainly was not over, not by a long shot. Back in the late 1980s, when I was working as both a fork-lift and a van driver for a company in the West Midlands, England town of Walsall, I heard a number of noteworthy stories pertaining to sightings of huge violent eels, which were said to roam the dark, winding canals of both the nearby city of Birmingham, and certain rural areas of the adjacent county of Staffordshire. Rather like some 1950s era street gang from the Bronx, they seemed to travel in packs, prepared to take on just about anything and everything that had the misfortune to cross their path.

One memorable account originated with a truck driver who recalled such a sighting somewhere in Birmingham on a summer's day in the late 1980s. It reportedly "shook the staff rigid" at a store that overlooked the stretch of canal in question. In this case, the mighty animal of the waters was described as being dark brown in color and said to be no less than 15 feet in length. Supposedly, it had briefly been seen by an employee who, completely mesmerized by its presence, watched it "circling" one area of the canal frequented by a large number of semi-tame ducks that the staff at the store regularly fed with bread during their daily lunch break. [1]

Equally intriguing was the story of Norman Dodd, who lived for many years in Scotland and who, in the 1970s, was a regular commuter to central England on business. It was at some point in the very hot and memorable summer of 1976 that he, too, had a remarkable encounter that took place in the Cannock Chase woods, which are no more than a 45-minute drive from the city of Birmingham and are a hotbed of seemingly never-ending supernatural strangeness. When I interviewed Dodd years later, he could not recall the exact location where the incident had taken place, but he *was* able to state with certainty that it was a small pool of no more than 20 feet by

30 feet that existed at the time, and that he is fairly sure was "not far from [the village of] Slitting Mill and perhaps a mile back into the [Cannock] Chase."

Dodd stated that he had parked his Ford Cortina on the grassy verge of the road that was adjacent to the pool and was munching on his lunch and reading a newspaper. "It was a bloody stifling day. Remember that summer, how hot it was? I remember swigging something to drink and having a bite when there was something moving right on the bank [of the pool]."

He had been startled to see a creature, which he estimated to be around six or seven feet long, slowly surface from the water and then proceeded to "bask" on the banks of the pool. "It wriggled like an eel," said Dodd, adding that "its body seemed to sort of shake or wobble as it moved." Dodd further explained that the animal had a serpent-like head, a "thick body," and an oily-colored skin. It seemed wholly unconcerned by his presence. "I know it saw me—or saw the car, definitely—because it looked right in this direction and then just went back to what it was up to: just laying there."

But what was most puzzling of all to the shocked Dodd was the realization that the animal seemed to have "flippers near the front, or little feet." He conceded that it may very well have had similar flippers or feet at its rear but that the "back-end never came right out of the water…" Dodd watched astonished, and not a little concerned, too, for at least 20 minutes, after which time the animal simply slid softly back into the pond and vanished from sight. He concluded: "I wondered how a small pond like that might feed an animal that big for food [sic]. But what about its feet or the flippers: does that mean it might have been able to go from pool to pool for fish and things?" These were questions that neither Dodd nor I could ever really answer. [2]

Python Panic!

In the early part of 2003, a story surfaced in the British press to the effect that the remains of a large dead python had been found in the same stretch of Birmingham canal where the giant eels were said to have been seen roaming years earlier. It was January 23 when the *Birmingham Evening Mail* newspaper splashed across its pages a sensational and eye-catching story titled *15-Foot Python Dead in*

Canal.

Steve Swingler, the journalist who broke the bizarre story, wrote: "Walkers, joggers and cyclists have been pounding a towpath in Edgbaston oblivious to a near-15ft Burmese Python lurking just feet away below the water. The giant reptile, capable of killing a child, was fished out of the canal near Rotten Park Road, Edgbaston by the RSPCA [Royal Society for the Prevention of Cruelty to Animals] yesterday. It had been spotted by a terrified passer-by." The beast, Swingler added, had only been dead for a very short time.

Inspector Rob Hartley, of the RSPCA Rescue Center in Barnes Hill, told the newspaper: "It's like something out of a horror movie. This thing is massive; we've never seen one this big before. It's a monster. We've measured it at fourteen and a half feet and up to 14 inches wide. It probably weighs at least 11 stone [154 pounds]. We don't know whether it simply got too big for someone to look after and they let it go free or it escaped."

The mystery, you may not be entirely surprised to learn, was never resolved. Were the old tales of giant eels on the loose actually based on sightings of a colony of pythons that had made the area their hidden home? That question would dog me for some time. [3]

"They Could Easily Have Swallowed a Child"

In 2007, a man named John Weatherley contacted me about the remarkable tale of his close-up encounter with giant eels: "I am British and live in Florida. My family and I came to Florida by sea from Australia in 1969. Our ship left Acapulco and sailed along the west coast towards the Panama Canal. It was the first week of July 1969. The sea was calm and we were cruising quite slowly because of congestion in the canal. As we cruised along the west coast of Costa Rica and Panama, we were about 7 or 8 miles from shore and just a few yards from the flotsam line. It was a clearly defined line of seaweed about 30 feet wide with odd bits of wood and the occasional small tree limb.

"We cruised along this path for several hours in bright sunshine between about 10:00 a.m. and 2:00 p.m. There were many fish visible and some very large turtles, but the significant sighting was huge eels. These creatures were always in pairs, and we saw a pair perhaps every 20 minutes or so. They averaged about 15 feet long and had a diameter of about one-and-a-half feet. They were khaki or olive in color and were identical to the eels for which I used to fish as a boy in my hometown of Canterbury Kent, except they were so large. They were lazily swimming very slowly along through the flotsam or just wallowing at the very surface. The ship was carrying about 1,200 passengers and most were on deck on this idyllic day, so the eels were seen by many people. Most were engaged in counting the enormous number of sharks, which were clearly visible around the ship. I wonder if you have any idea what species of eel these were? They could easily have swallowed a child or a small adult." [4]

I wondered, too, and I duly sent John a bunch of photos of eels known to inhabit the very waters in question, but he advised me that the beasts he saw were far stranger: "Thanks for the inputs, Nick. Unfortunately they did not add a great deal to the identity of the eels that I and my fellow passengers saw all those years ago. The images are still very clear in my mind's eye. I am not much of an ichthyologist or zoologist for that matter, being a retired communications engineer by profession, so I can only speculate and very possibly be in error. However, I would suggest that since we only saw these creatures in pairs that possibly they had come to the surface for mating as I believe do some other relatively deep water species.

"Also, every moray eel picture that I have ever seen usually depicted a fish with a spotted or patterned body. These were not like that but a uniform smooth light khaki or even green/mustard color. Also the snout of the moray is quite pronounced. If memory serves me correctly, the ones we saw had a more rounded nose. I do not recall the eyes being specifically prominent either, although we are now stretching my memory a bit. I only wish I had access to a good telescopic lens for my camera at the time." [5]

The Beasts of Birmingham

Time and time again, controversial and sensational stories like this one managed to come my way, suggesting that truly giant eels were indeed a reality and might even be lurking within the waters of our major cities and towns, too. But it was not until August 2009 that I was able to undertake a first-hand investigation of this fishy controversy, only a couple of days after my trip to Rhayader. Here's how it all began.

In March 2009, I received an email from a man named Gordon Moseley, who claimed to have seen, some three months earlier, a true leviathan of the deep: an eel some 17 or 18 feet in length, dwelling within a stretch of Birmingham canal only a quarter of a mile or so from where the body of the goliath-sized dead python was hauled out six years earlier.

"I couldn't really take it in," Moseley told me later by telephone. "I knew what I was looking at, but couldn't believe it. I just looked and looked; I never did anything but stare. And then it went under the water, after probably a minute and I lost it. But, it was massive." Of course, having heard Moseley's story, and realizing that the waters of Birmingham were apparently *still* home to such marauding monsters, I knew that I had to make a trip out to the area and see what was afoot. [6]

In stark contrast to the weather in Rhayader a few days earlier, it was a beautiful, hot August afternoon when I when I arrived to check out Birmingham's legendary eels. I borrowed a friend's two-man dinghy, loaded it into the back of my dad's Fiat, and was soon on my way—after the parting remark from my dad: "Take care of my bloody car!"

One specific stretch of the canal appeared to be home to the nightmarish creatures, according to several independent witnesses who had informed the local media. That stretch can be found near Rotten Park Road in an area of Birmingham called Edgbaston. Rotten Park Road is only a short distance from the site of Gordon Moseley's encounter, and it is very close to where the dead python surfaced in 2003, making the whole investigation even more intriguing and worthwhile.

But before I could take to the waters, I had another port of call. Purely on a whim, two days before I decided to embark on the great eel hunt, I phoned Birmingham's BBC Radio WM, which regularly invited me on their shows whenever there was local high strangeness to report on, and told them of my planned excursion. Luckily, the researcher at the station I spoke with practically foamed at the mouth with excitement at the idea that there might be a West Midlands equivalent of the Loch Ness Monster skulking around the area. And as a result, I was eagerly invited on one of WM's afternoon talk-shows. Well, if ever I doubted the existence of the great gods of synchronicity, now was most certainly the time for me to offer them a formal apology. After I discussed the stories of the giant eels of Birmingham with the radio-host, the telephone-lines were opened up for people all across the West Midlands to call in and offer comments, thoughts, and opinions, which they certainly did. Most just had a few tidbits of data to relate, primarily relating to sightings of large fish, rather than huge eels or giant snakes.

It transpired, however, that one soft-spoken caller who identified himself as a Mr. Sykes had more than a few tantalizing bits of data to impart. Two decades earlier, Sykes had been a police constable serving in the very area that I would be exploring. Of course, I cannot say with absolute certainty that the caller was not a fantasist or even an outright liar capitalizing on the story for some odd and obscure reason of his own. Nor can I deny the possibility that, because the planned interview was widely advertised on-air for two days, it might have given Sykes time to create a faked story. I have to say, however, that this is definitely not the way he came across on the airwaves. And so, for that reason alone, I feel it's only right to share his whole story with you in these pages.

Sykes' tone and character suggested that he was the sort of friendly, elderly upholder of the law that barely seems to exist in today's world. In short and simple terms, he was the type of copper who would have genially helped an old lady across a busy street 50 years ago. Not like today's emotionless and unsmiling breed who would most likely have tasered the very same old lady for mistakenly putting out her garbage for collection on the wrong day, or for forgetting to take off her shoes while negotiating airport security.

Sykes had actually heard two tales of giant eels seen on this stretch of canal, both of which surfaced, he thought anyway, around 1979 or 1980. In each case, the witnesses reported seeing large creatures—*very* large creatures—the first, amazingly, around 20 feet in length, the other slightly shorter, but both very dark in color. I remarked on the air that if the physical details described in the first encounter were not exaggerations on the part of the witness, then this was without any doubt a true monster of the deep.

Notably, Sykes said that although he was not the investigating officer in either case, he recalled that around the same time the eels were seen, there had been a spate of mysterious disappearances of pet rabbits and cats in the same area. And while some of Sykes' colleagues had attributed this to the work of sadists or particularly cruel kids, there had been brief talk back at the police station that "it was the eels' doing." And there was one other ominous story that Sykes recalled and related as I, and the show's host, listened to intently in almost complete silence. At the height of the rabbit disappearances and the two eel encounters, someone had contacted the police station Sykes was working at with a remarkable tale.

"It was a local chap, in his twenties," said Sykes. "The chap hadn't been married long and had just bought a house around here." According to our storyteller, the man quickly telephoned the police after hearing a huge commotion in his small backyard in the early hours one morning. The wooden fence at the foot of the yard was partially smashed down, a large area of grass had been squashed flat, and something had broken into his rabbit hutch, utterly destroying it in the process. Needless to say, by the time the man got downstairs and raced into the yard, there was no sign of the unknown intruder— and, unfortunately, no sign of a single bunny, either.

Continuing on with his tale, Sykes theorized that the eels, hungry for food, had probably elected to leave the confines of the canal and had, under the protective cover of darkness, slithered around the yards of the nearby homes in search of a tasty rabbit or several. Well, it was just about as good a theory as any, I thought. And it was downright disturbing to think that such fantastic beasts might secretly be on the loose in and around Birmingham, mercilessly prowling the winding waters, back-roads, and alleyways by night. As far as Sykes knew, this unsettling incident was never resolved. Mercifully, however, no other sightings surfaced, and a rigorous search of the canal failed to find anything conclusive. For the police, the case was closed.

Setting Sail

I figured that if giant eels really *had* made the canals of Birmingham their home and were still there years later, then the most advantageous of all times to find them would be in the early hours of the morning, when the good folk of the area were all in their beds, when the bustling, noisy traffic was at a minimum, and when darkness and relative silence had firmly blanketed and embraced the whole area. It might just be then, I reasoned, that my quarry would surface, hungry for the massive amounts of food that were surely required to fill and fuel their gigantic forms. So I settled in at a nearby pub for a few hours, quaffed some good cold lager, downed a plate of steaming hot fish and chips, patiently waited for closing-time to come along, and then trudged back to the canal to engage in a bit of night-time creature seeking.

I returned to where I had parked my dad's car, pulled the dinghy out of the trunk, inflated it, and set to work. Although I had a powerful flashlight with me, I certainly didn't want to give away my presence by illuminating the canal as if it was daytime, at this stage, at least, and possibly end up spooking whatever might have been lurking in the water. So by the light of nothing but a bright and welcome moon, I carefully and quietly lowered myself into the dinghy and began to paddle lightly.

Since time immemorial, brave mariners of the sea have required some sort of musical accompaniment to keep their minds stimulated and firmly on the task in-hand. Thus it was that I elected to quietly sing a traditional, touching and romantic shanty known to all of those intrepid souls who have ever sailed the harsh oceans of our planet, "Friggin' in the Riggin'," which received a notorious injection of publicity in the late 1970s when the Sex Pistols recorded their own memorable, punk rock-themed version of the old expletive-loaded song.

For at least three hours I traveled the still waters of the canal, occasionally hearing the eerie screams of the local fox population, and more than once scraping the bottom of the dinghy on unknown things below, in all probability discarded bicycle frames or shopping-carts—the latter, rather curiously, can always seemingly be found within the many canals of the British Isles, and usually after closing-time on a Friday night. Now and again, I pointed the flashlight at the dark waters and turned it on. This actually proved to be quite a profitable action, as I saw countless fish, and some of impressive sizes, too, briefly caught in the sudden glare. But the monster eels, if they really were swimming the canal, consistently eluded me.

I knew very well that even if such beasts *had* been present in the 1970s and 1980s, it certainly didn't mean that their offspring were still around 30 years later, although the story of Gordon Moseley certainly suggested they might have been. Perhaps the inevitably of old age, or a lack of regular nourishment in the vast quantities that would surely be required to sustain such creatures had utterly doomed them, and they ultimately became sustenance themselves for the many and varied other creatures that inhabited the canal. Nevertheless, I felt that I had at least given it a go. And, admittedly, I did have some additional, interesting testimony, courtesy of Police Constable Sykes and Gordon Moseley, to add to my burgeoning database on British-based giant eel stories. So, I headed back to the bank of the canal, then to the car, and was soon bound for my dad's for a few more days, before heading on to that year's Weird Weekend gig.

Weighing the Evidence

There were a number of highly vexing questions that still required answering—if they could even be answered. What were the odds, I wondered, of a dead python popping up in 2003, in the *exact* same stretch of canal where giant eels were said to be lurking more than 20 years earlier and also six years later? Could it possibly be that the initial reports from the 1970s and 1980s were actually also of giant pythons, and *not* of huge eels, after all? Was mistaken identity the key to this weird puzzle? It would certainly have been very much easier for snakes, rather than eels, to slither along on solid ground in search of a few rabbits and cats. But, if so, then that was highly problematic, too.

First, it suggested that someone had to have been secretly breeding pythons in the area for many years, and to have been surreptitiously releasing them into the waters of the canals around Birmingham, all without ever getting caught or identified in the process. But why do so? Second, the idea that such beasts could even *begin* to cope with the less than hospitable British weather for any lengthy period of time was highly unlikely. Actually, it was all beyond unlikely. And, certainly, each and every experienced breeder of snakes would be well aware of that singular and stark fact. So, again, why release them into the canals of Birmingham, where they would surely be faced with naught but quick and distinctly unpleasant deaths? Absolutely nothing about this story made any sense at all.

There was, of course, another possibility: that totally against all the odds, and utterly flying in the face of both accepted wisdom and the tumultuous British weather, a colony of giant pythons—innocently mistaken by more than a few for huge eels—was indeed living in stealth in the canals, grasslands, woods, and undergrowth that flourished in and around the city of Birmingham, and had done so since the late 1970s and up until at least 2009. I have to say, I found this scenario extremely difficult, if not overwhelmingly impossible, to accept. I also realized, however, that the likelihood of two distinctly different types of creature—although arguably somewhat very similar in *initial* appearance—could be in residence in the exact same stretch of canal was even more credibility stretching. I could only conclude that if pythons *had* been on the loose for more than 20 years in and around Birmingham, then this would be a discovery of unparalleled proportions.

Yet, if the 2003 case merely involved a single escaped python, and if the earlier reports really were of giant eels after all, then the gods of synchronicity were certainly playing some decidedly odd games by allowing both beasts to flourish in precisely the same locale. Today, the mystery of Birmingham's massive eels and huge snakes is arguably far stranger than it was when the affair began all those years ago. The day will surely come, however, when I shall return to the old, dark city, and to its mysterious and winding waters and their strange secrets, and once again seek out the creatures of that curious stretch of ancient canal.

Neil's Supernatural Serpent

There is a very odd sequel to the curious affair of the giant eels and/or snakes of Birmingham, and the wormy beast of Rhayader, all of which caught my firm attention in the summer of 2009. Only a few days after my night time expedition around the canals of Birmingham was complete, I made an early morning, five-hour car journey with fellow Fortean Dr. Dan Holdsworth at the wheel of his vehicle to the home in Woolfardisworthy, Devonshire, of great friend and fellow monster-seeker Jon Downes, at whose annual Weird Weekend gig I was due to speak. My dad had said, in stern tones, that his car had by now suffered quite enough stresses and strains born out of my monster-hunts in Birmingham and Wales. Also on the roster for the weekend was my good mate Neil Arnold, one of the U.K.'s leading researchers of cryptozoological and Fortean phenomena, and the author of such books as *Paranormal London* and *Monster!* It so transpires that while at the event Neil had a paranormal and nightmarish experience involving nothing less than a large, terrifying snake.

"Being a full-time monster hunter," Neil wrote shortly after the encounter occurred, "should be about traipsing through forests in search of strange creatures: large, exotic cats in local woods, elusive critters in remote lakes, peculiar insects, escaped wallabies, a bit of 'Nessie' here, and giant birds there. Yet what happened to me at this years' Weird Weekend was the most terrifying moment of my life. ..

"Myself and my girlfriend [and, now, Neil's wife] Jemma were put up by Jon and Co. at the lovely Braund-Phillips household at Bucks Cross. The night I lectured on weird zooform creatures—from the female molesting "green underpants" to London's vampires—we retired to our room and nodded off. At 3:00 a.m. I woke up and was fully aware that an enormous snake was in the bedroom. It was pale in color with beige blotches over its head. The head of this thing suggested a snake around 25 feet in length, as its head was the size of a flattened football. Its beady eyes peered at me in the gloom and then it struck. It was a constricting snake, for when its jaws clamped on my right arm, there was no venom excreted, merely a heavy weight. I leapt up in absolute horror, screaming. I yanked my arm from its vice-like grip but then it proceeded to coil around my right leg."

The terror had barely begun for Neil and Jemma: "At this point Jemma was yelling my name, unaware of the horror that had coiled around me. I made for the door, but it dragged me back, heavily grazing my knees as they made contact with the carpet. I wrenched my leg from its grasp only to see it coil around Jemma's legs. I pulled at her, and also attempted to open the door. Suddenly the horror dissipated and it was over. Jemma never saw the spectral snake, but recalled how she'd felt constricted in the night and smothered.

"People will tell me it was a dream," wrote Neil, concluding his account. "However, Richard Freeman and Jon both know that in the past I've been attacked in my bed by several vampyric amorphous blobs. On these occasions I was awake. This time I may well have drifted into some astral place, but that thing was huge. And, the next day I showed Richard, his girlfriend Lisa, and Nick Redfern the cuts on my knees. Strangely, Richard's girlfriend Lisa recalled how a couple of years previous whilst staying at the B&B, she'd felt constricted in the night and woke to find bruises down her arms. Now, I know there's no giant snake on the loose in Bideford, and I believe that what I saw had something to do with my lecture. It's happened before and it will probably happen again. But where these things come from, I do not know, but in every case of being attacked I've either been drained of energy or blood. True vampires? Who knows, but if anyone debates as to whether psychic backlash is for real, I had the marks to prove it." [7]

Before driving to Jon Downes' abode with Dan Holdsworth, I had spent a couple of days doggedly pursuing, and deeply musing upon, terrible water-beasts resembling giant worms, huge eels, and massive snakes across both mid Wales and the city of Birmingham, England. Did this very fact result in the manifestation of a true mind-monster of a very similar nature and appearance that briefly, and horrifyingly, entered our realm of existence, and scared the "you know what" out of Neil and Jemma on that night in the centuries-old locale of Woolfardisworthy? *Was I responsible?* Having thought deeply about this menacing matter, it's a dark possibility that even to this very day I simply cannot bring myself to fully deny—although I earnestly wish I could do precisely that.

Chapter 4
Winged Things of Wisconsin

"It looked just like the *Jeepers Creepers* monster."

The Ultimate Sky Beast

There can surely be very few people reading this book who have not at least heard of the legendary Mothman of Point Pleasant, West Virginia, that so terrorized the town and its surrounding areas between November 1966 and December 1967. Its enigmatic exploits were chronicled in *The Mothman Prophecies,* the 2002 hit Hollywood movie starring Richard Gere, that was named after the monumentally mysterious and entertaining book of the same title written by the legendary John Keel. [1]

A gargoyle-like, winged monster with a pair of large, glowing or reflecting, red eyes, the Mothman's daunting appearance seemingly came out of nowhere and, some say, ultimately culminated in high tragedy and death. But what, exactly, *was* the Mothman of Point Pleasant? And how did the legend begin? To try and answer those questions we have to go back to the night of November 12, 1966, when five grave-diggers working in a cemetery in the nearby town of Clendenin were shocked to see what they described as a "brown human shape with wings" rise ominously out of the thick, surrounding trees and soar away into the night sky. Not a good sign. [2]

Three days later, the unearthly beast surfaced once again. It was at the witching-hour when Roger and Linda Scarberry and Steve and Mary Mallette—two young, married couples from Point Pleasant— were passing the time away by cruising around town. After a while, the foursome decided to drive out to the West Virginia Ordnance Works, which was basically an abandoned explosives factory that had been used to make TNT during the Second World War, and which was situated just a few miles north of Point Pleasant in the McClintic Wildlife Station.

As they drove around the old factory, the four were puzzled and frightened to see in the shadows what looked like two red lights pointing in their direction. These were no normal lights, however.

Rather, all four were shocked and horrified to discover that, in reality, the lights were the glowing, self-illuminating red eyes of a huge animal that, as Roger Scarberry later recalled, was "shaped like a Mothman, but bigger, maybe six and a half or seven feet tall, with big wings folded against its back."

Not surprisingly, the four fled the area at high speed. Unfortunately for the Scarberrys and the Mallettes, however, the beast was far from finished with them and decided to pursue the four. As they sped off for the safety of Point Pleasant, the winged monster took to the skies and shadowed their vehicle's every movement until it reached the city limits. The two couples then raced to the sheriff's office and told their astounding story to Deputy Millard Halstead, who later stated that: "I've known these kids all their lives. They'd never been in any trouble and they were really scared that night. I took them seriously." And even though a search of the area by Halstead did not solve the mystery, the macabre Mothman was soon set to return. [3]

"On the day after the Scraberry-Mallette sighting," wrote Janet and Colin Bord of the on-going Mothman affair, "Mothman showed himself to Marcella Bennett of Point Pleasant, who at 9 p.m. on 16 November was visiting a friend living in the TNT area. As she got out of the car, a grey figure with red eyes seemed to rise from the ground behind it. He was staring at her, and she stood as if transfixed while her companions ran for the house. Somehow she picked up her young daughter, whom she had dropped in fear, and got into the house." [4]

And the incidents just kept on surfacing.

Early on the morning of November 25, yet another remarkable encounter with the mysterious beast took place, as John Keel noted: "Thomas Ury was driving along Route 62 just north of the TNT area when he noticed a tall, grey, manlike figure standing in a field by the road. 'Suddenly it spread a pair of wings,' Ury said, 'and took off straight up, like a helicopter. It veered over my convertible and began going in circles three telephone poles high. It kept flying right over my car even though I was doing about seventy-five." [5]

Over the next few days and nights more sightings surfaced, including that of Ruth Foster of nearby Charleston, who saw the winged monster after sunset in her garden: "It was tall with big red eyes that popped out of its face. My husband is six-feet-one and this bird looked about the same height or a little shorter, maybe." [6]

Needless to say, the local media had an absolute field day with the sensational story that had fallen into its lap. Tales of what were referred to as the "Bird-Monster" hit the headlines, and both skeptics and local police ensured their views and opinions on the matter were widely known. Robert L. Smith, an associate professor of wildlife biology in the Division of Forestry at West Virginia University, expressed his opinion that the Mothman was nothing stranger than a large Sandhill Crane. This hardly satisfied the witnesses, however. In response to Smith's assertion, Thomas Ury came straight to the point and said: "I've seen big birds, but I've never seen anything like this." [7]

As for the Point Pleasant police, they offered stern warnings to any and all would-be monster-hunters contemplating seeking out the mysterious creature. As the *Herald Dispatch* newspaper noted: "Sheriff [George] Johnson said he would arrest anybody caught with a loaded gun in the area after dark [and] warned that the scores of persons searching the abandoned powerhouse in the TNT area after dark risked possible serious injury." [8]

In the weeks and months that followed, further encounters with the bizarre beast were reported, but, they were all overshadowed by a terrible and tragic event that occurred on December 15, 1967. On that day Point Pleasant's Silver Bridge (so named after its aluminum-colored paint) that spanned the Ohio River and connected Point Pleasant to Gallipolis, Ohio, collapsed into the river, tragically claiming nearly 50 lives. Interestingly, after the disaster at the Silver Bridge occurred, encounters with the Mothman came to a grinding halt, other than the occasional sighting that might take place in the years and decades that followed. And while a down-to-earth explanation for the collapse of the bridge most certainly circulated— namely, that a fatal flaw in a single eye-bar in a suspension chain was the chief culprit—many saw, and many still continue to see, the cause of the disaster as being somehow linked with the ominous and overwhelming presence of the Mothman. Whether the Mothman *was* the cause of the event, or if its presence was meant to try and warn people of an impending disaster is an issue that divides researchers of the phenomenon, nearly 50 years later. [9]

And still the specter of the Mothman continues to loom large, decades after Point Pleasant became enveloped in high tragedy and macabre death. In fact, there's evidence to suggest that while the Mothman may have largely left Point Pleasant behind, it has never really gone away completely. Rather, it still seems to surface from time to time, always ready to astound and amaze those whose path it decides to cross, no matter where they might live.

The Other Mothmen

Around 9:30 p.m. on an April 1994 evening, eighteen-year-old Brian Canfield was driving home to the isolated settlement of Camp One, which was situated near the town of Buckley, Washington State. All was completely normal until the engine on Brian's pickup truck suddenly died, the vehicle's interior lights went out, and the car came to a halt. Curiously, the vehicle's headlights were not affected, which was fortunate (or unfortunate, depending on your perspective of what happened next), since they allowed a terror-stricken Brian to see an approximately nine-foot-tall, winged monster descend from the skies and practically fill the road in front of him. The creature, Brian later recalled, had blue-tinted fur, yellowish eyes, the feet of a bird, and sharp, straight teeth. It also possessed a huge pair of wings, the veritable hallmark of the Mothman.

Commenting on the very unnerving experience, Brian said: "It was standing there staring at me like it was resting, like it didn't know what to think. I was scared; it raised the hair on me. I didn't feel threatened. I just felt out of place. I'm really not into this stuff. It boggles my mind really hard core. I really can't explain it. It's weird, definitely weird. I don't like it. Usually this stuff happens to someone else." [10]

There are even claims that Mothman-style beasts were seen in the immediate period leading up to the collapse on August 1, 2007, of Mississippi's I-35W bridge, an event that left 13 people dead and more than 100 injured, after countless vehicles plunged into the waters at the height of the evening rush-hour. [11]

And an in-depth study of both ancient and modern day folklore clearly demonstrates that numerous cultures all around the world have tales of dark and dangerous winged monsters that sound eerily like the infamous Mothman of Point Pleasant, West Virginia. England is home to the Owlman, a *very* Mothman-like creature that is said to inhabit the dark woods surrounding Mawnan Church, Cornwall. It was the subject of Jon Downes' award-winning book *The Owlman and Others.* [12] Then there is the devil-like gargoyle of the ancient town of Glastonbury, Somerset, England that, rumor says, guards the final resting place of the legendary King Arthur [13]; and London's very own flying wonder, the Brentford Griffin that plagued Brentford in the mid 1980s. [14] Moving further afield, Japan is home to a grotesque bird-like demon known as the Tengu, a "bat-winged baboon" called Popobawa travels the wilds of Zanzibar, and throughout Scandinavia tales circulate of a giant terrifying owl known as Skovman. [15]

Whether or not these bizarre flying monsters are merely the products of imagination, mythology, or mistaken identity, or if they represent some form of very real and ominous portent to death and disaster remains unknown. Needless to say, with no hard answers forthcoming, the legend, mystery, and fear of the Mothman still thrive today. And I can attest to that personally. In early September 2009, I headed off to the wilds of Wisconsin in search of the Badger State's very own winged equivalent of the Mothman.

Searching the Skies

The period September 5-9, 2009, was a decidedly strange one. Late on the night of the 5th, I watched for the umpteenth time the 1997 horror-movie, *Mimic,* which tells the story of man-sized cockroaches, cunningly disguised as black-cloaked human beings by pulling their dark wings around them, that live deep within the maze-like bowels of the New York subway system. They feast upon the city's unfortunates, vagrants, and just about anyone and everyone else who has the distinctly bad luck to cross their cold-hearted paths after the sun has set. [16]

Twelve hours after the film ended, I was sitting in a departure lounge at Dallas-Fort Worth International Airport awaiting a flight to Minneapolis and a subsequent flight to Wisconsin. The reason: to film an episode of the History Channel's cryptozoology-driven series, *MonsterQuest.* [17] The subject of the episode was giant, bat-like beasts said to inhabit the wilder parts of the state. I couldn't help but think there wasn't really that much difference between the man-sized cockroaches of *Mimic* that had kept me entertained the night before, John Keel's Mothman, and the giant bat-beasts of Wisconsin that I was now all set to pursue. Perhaps, I mused, I would uncover evidence suggesting that something terrifying had been feasting upon the good folk of America's Dairyland.

A couple of days before I left for Wisconsin, the producer of the episode, Anna Mikelson, telephoned me to ask what sort of equipment I might consider to be suitable for our adventure. It did not take me long to deduce that *MonsterQuest* regarded the Wisconsin Mothman as nothing stranger than a particularly large type of owl. And with that hypothesis in mind, Anna told me they intended to have me gadding around the woods playing recordings of owl hoots at full blast, while cameras, night-vision equipment, and more would record and catalog my every movement— and, hopefully, the Mothman's every movement, too. This, then, was going to be an investigation of the technical and scientific kind. Since I consider the Mothman to be a paranormal creature, as opposed to one of flesh and blood, I suggested to Anna that we try and invoke the dastardly beast via foul callings to the underworld. My suggestion was met with mystified silence. So, okay, science rather than sorcery it would be.

But why, you might ask, should I be looking for the Mothman in Wisconsin in the first place? Wouldn't it have made more sense for *MonsterQuest* to focus on the creature's original haunt of Point Pleasant, West Virginia? Well, yes, the team certainly *did* do precisely that. As Anna Mikelson told me when I was first approached to appear on the show, the plan was to target various parts of the United States where the aerial monster and its ilk had been seen—including Point Pleasant—and see what evidence we could come up with. As for why Wisconsin was chosen, well, that was very simple and quite justified. Back in September 2006, a nightmarish encounter occurred in La Crosse, Wisconsin, that was investigated by a friend of mine, local author and journalist named Linda Godfrey, who is renowned for her dedicated and thorough research into Dogman- and werewolf-like entities seen throughout the state and elsewhere, as described in her books *The Beast of Bray Road, Hunting the American Werewolf,* and *The Michigan Dogman.* [18]

"Imagine driving down a dark country road, minding your own business," writes Godfrey, "when suddenly a screaming, man-sized creature with bat-like wings flies at your windshield, stares in at you, then swoops upwards into the night sky. It happened to a 53-year-old La Crosse man who prefers to be known only by his Cherokee name, Wohali, and the man's 25-year-old son." As Linda learned, terror and disbelief were quickly overwhelmed by something else: sudden illness. After seeing the creature, both men immediately felt violently sick, to the extent that Wohali's son was forced to quickly bring the truck to a halt at the side of the road so that he could vomit into a nearby ditch. [19]

It was curious cases and events such as this one that led me to believe that seeking out the Wisconsin Mothman in conventional fashion was utterly doomed to failure. But, regardless, I agreed to head northwards in search of the ominous truth. As so often happens in such situations, things totally failed to run smoothly. After a lengthy delay in getting airborne, caused by "two broken light bulbs and a knob that has fallen off a control panel," I finally took my seat, only to have the woman sitting next to me immediately spill a near-full venti-sized Starbucks coffee all over my black jeans. This was not a good start. And it only got progressively worse as the day went on.

When I landed at my connection point, there was a message on my cell phone from a man named Mark Peterson, who was also taking part in the show. He was asking me not to make my second flight, as it was actually going to be far easier and much quicker for him to meet me at my first port of call, and for us to then make a couple of hours' drive to the hotel. Well, that was all fine with me. At least, it was until I learned that failing to get on a connecting flight without informing the relevant airline was considered by its staff to be a threat to the national security of the United States of America.

Whoever knew that the Mothman was capable of provoking so much trouble?

And as a result, the airline in question, which will go unnamed, summarily and speedily cancelled my return flight to Dallas. No doubt they were thinking that my monster-hunting excursion was a cover for some nefarious Al Qaeda sponsored plot to provoke mayhem and destruction in the Land of the (now less than) Free. Thankfully, however, a quick and grovelling apology from a representative of *MonsterQuest* smoothed things over with a particularly tedious and emotionless automaton at the airline, and my tickets were duly restored to their former worth with lightning speed. But I'll bet that bloody airline now has a file on me as thick as a book, I thought.

Finally it was time to hit the road. With his cowboy hat, boots, and ever-present wad of tobacco firmly embedded in his jaw, Mark was a definite outdoors type with an expert knowledge of wildlife and wilderness. He was the perfect person to have along for the expedition. Mark and I chatted genially as he drove the several hours to our base-camp, which was the town of Winona. An interesting debate developed about Bigfoot during the course of the journey, in which Mark, a believer, opined that it is possibly a migratory creature, and one that follows certain trails in search of vital salts, minerals, food, and more.

Mark also had an opinion about the original reports of the Mothman from Point Pleasant. It was a weird opinion, too: he believed the Mothman was nothing stranger than someone fooling around with a hang-glider. Needless to say, we agreed to disagree on that one, and we passed the rest of the journey making cryptozoological conversation and taking in the wonderfully lush scenery: the woods, the hills, and the seemingly endless, rolling fields. But there was one other thing Mark wanted to say.

Later that night, as we ate dinner, Mark told me that while undertaking research for *MonsterQuest*, he learned that Wisconsin's Native American Indians had a long tradition of giant, winged birds haunting the state's huge Trempealeau Mountain, which was to be one of our major points of investigation. And then, with dinner and drinks eagerly devoured, it was time to head to our respective rooms, await the arrival of the rest of the team who were all flying in on a redeye (*not* a glowing red-eye!), and learn what tomorrow would bring our way.

The Quest Begins

Well, the first thing that the next day provided was a blanket of fog. Impenetrable scarcely described it. As I took an early morning stroll around outside the hotel, I almost expected to see the wild, blazing eyes of the Hound of the Baskervilles itself come looming out of the dense gray and white mass that had descended upon the entire town of Winona.

When I walked back into the lobby, a female voice from the

nearby breakfast room asked: "Are you Nick?" I confirmed that, yes, I was Nick. The questioner was the producer, Anna, who immediately admitted to me that, as this was her very first experience of working as a producer on *MonsterQuest*, she was somewhat mystified by the whole thing. I could scarcely disagree. It was, after all, a decidedly strange way to pass one's days and earn one's living. She then introduced me to the rest of the team. Andrew was a quiet vegetarian and the resident sound-guy, while Jim, the cameraman, was an expert on all things technological.

After I finished my breakfast of hot tea, and toast and jam, we loaded up the vehicles with the cameras, night-vision equipment, snacks, drinks, and much more, and hit the road for Trempealeau Mountain, which is protected by the luscious Perrot State Park, so named after Nicolas Perrot, an early French explorer. [20] In a nice bit of irony, as we headed out of town to our location, we crossed an old fog-shrouded bridge that could easily have doubled for the ill-fated construction that collapsed in Point Pleasant, West Virginia, all those years earlier. As we slowly negotiated the thick fog, I scanned the highest points of the bridge for anything black, winged, and glowing-eyed that might be looming over us. It was not to be, however.

Then, after preliminary filming to secure background data on me and Mark, as well as our thoughts on what the original Mothman might or might not have been, it was time for the show to hit full throttle. A canoe was carefully lowered into the water, and, having climbed in, we paddled along the waters that led to the mountain. Upon reaching our quarry, the hardest part began: a near-killer and practically vertical climb up the mountain in what felt like 100-degree heat. A certain pasty, pale, skinny Brit did not fare at all well. Even Mark, the experienced outdoorsman, suffered noticeably. But we finally made it, gulped down a couple of bottles of water each, and patiently awaited the arrival of a helicopter and crew that had been hired to take some aerial shots of us "in action," so to speak.

The panoramic view was truly amazing. All around us was a vast expanse of gigantic peaks, flowing rivers, and near-impenetrable woods. In terms of the reported Mothman presence, certainly the most interesting thing was that near the very top of the peak we had just scaled were many large trees, pretty much lacking in any foliage, but with large, thick branches that hung precariously over the side of the mountain. Both Mark and I thought these branches would make for perfect take off points for any large, winged predator wanting to take to the skies, and make use of the thermals to search the surrounding areas for a bit of tasty prey. The helicopter got its shots, we gulped down even more water and downed a few power bars, and then made our way back down the mountainside for the next sequence.

Thankfully, with our mammoth climb and descent over, the next stage of the expedition had to wait until darkness had descended upon the woods and the mountain. So, after getting lots of extra footage of us roaming around and pretending to look as investigative as we conceivably could, we took advantage of a very welcome dinner break to revitalize our pummeled blood sugar. Then came the night. The plan was, in theory, a very easy one. In practice, however, it was not without its difficulties.

Countless original witnesses to the Mothman had said that the creature seemingly possessed a pair of self-illuminated glowing or highly reflecting eyes. So Anna's idea was for us to head out into the wilds of the area around 9:00 or 10:00 p.m. to try and film some footage of the eyes of the many deer that certainly called the area home, and to compare the eye reflection of these very down-to-earth animals with what had been reported in relation to the Mothman. In other words, the plan was to try and determine if people were actually mistaking the Mothman for something else entirely, such as deer half-seen and half-hidden in the dense shadows. It was unfortunate, but hardly a surprise to any of us, that the deer were not exactly the most cooperative of creatures and, aside from a couple of occasions when we did secure some good eye reflection footage, they kept their distance. But *some* footage, we all reasoned, was far better than *no* footage at all. And then we were hotel-bound and ready for yet another day.

Jeepers Creepers!

On returning to the hotel, something very interesting happened. I was hardly ready for bed on my return, so I elected to hang out in a small eatery over the road from our place of slumber, where I chatted genially with the bar staff, mainly about what on Earth a Brit was doing in Winona on a Wednesday night, and downed a few very welcome cold drinks in the process. Well, when I told them about what was afoot, one of the staff reeled off a very memorable story told to her some years earlier by her mother, and which had involved the girl's grandmother.

It had been late one night in the 1960s when the then forty-something woman had reportedly seen a "big flying animal" lurking on a rooftop on the fringes of Winona. The beast, I was told, was perched precariously, "with its wings out," and glared menacingly at the poor woman as she raced by, utterly scared out of her wits by the presence of the unholy monster. "It looked just like the *Jeepers Creepers* monster" were the last memorable words said to me on this particular affair. No elaborate tale, just a few choice facts that the waitress remembered having been told by her mother seven or eight years earlier. I had to consider the reality of the situation: it seemed highly coincidental that I should just happen to be in the right place at the right time to hear such a tale. Was this just a case of a bit of leg-pulling on the part of the staff, bored out of their brains on a quiet, Wednesday night in sleepy Winona? I can never say for sure; however, that certainly was not the impression that developed in my mind, I have to confess. [21]

And that was not all. Just over the road from the hotel was a McDonalds, where, the next morning, after being asked the by now near ubiquitous question—"What's an Englishman doing way out here?"—the staff crowded around me and, again, a story was duly delivered. In this particular case, it involved a truck driver "who came in here a few years back" saying his vehicle had been buzzed by a "giant eagle" as he approached the town. So the story went, the man watched amazed as the huge, winged monster flew to the top of a large tree-covered peak practically next door to our hotel, and issued forth a loud, shrill scream. Again, I can't eliminate the possibility that fabrication was at work here, but there were no half-hidden sniggers. In actuality, when coupled with the 2006 story of Wohali and his son, which featured in the finished *MonsterQuest* production, these two stories suggested that sightings of, and encounters with, unidentified winged things were surprisingly common in and around little Winona.

The next afternoon we discovered a truly gargantuan mushroom in the woods, next to which sat two of the fattest and largest toads it has ever been my delight to encounter. I commented for the camera that if the locals were making hearty meals out of such gargantuan mushrooms, and licking such immense toads in the process, then it was no surprise at all they were seeing the Mothman! That scene did not make the final show, unfortunately.

Joking aside, we had one more task to perform before I could say for certain I would have enough to make that month's house payment, courtesy of the History Channel. It was time to try and reel-in the Mothman by blasting the neighborhood with the recorded vocalizations of various and sundry owls, all broadcast at truly ear-splitting volume. Now, I'm always one for cranking up the CD-player and pummeling the neighbors with a bit of Megadeth or Motorhead, but to hear the hoots of an owl sounding like they are coming out of the speakers at a Slayer gig is not much fun at all, even for me, whose ear-drums have been battered and bruised for decades. But, if the Mothman was to be encouraged to come forth, then it just had to be done.

Thus it was that late at night and by the light of nothing but a bright moon, we stood near the base of the huge mountain, staring upwards in awe and anticipation. As Anna looked on with a mixture of excitement and trepidation, and as Andrew and Jim began to record the action, Mark let loose with the owl calls. "Deafening" is a word that scarcely describes the situation in which we found ourselves. Somewhat amusingly, I could not help but notice that within the couple of houses that stood on the fringes of Trempeleau Mountain, lights were suddenly turned on. No doubt, the hysterical owners were thinking that they were very possibly about to become the monster-bird's next tasty meal. Actually, the whole experience was quite instructive. After all, if there really *were* giant, flying beasts in the area, then broadcasting such screeches might not have been such a bad idea after all. And, I have to say, it was somewhat of a tense time as Mark, with the benefit of advanced night-vision equipment provided to us by *MonsterQuest*, and I carefully scanned the skies for any dark and large, shadowy forms that might be circling above and attempting to seek out what it was that was making those screeches. If our quarry was out there, it elected to remain in the thick woods that were the veritable hallmark of the steep, imposing mountainside.

Frankly, I felt that far more time should have been applied to securing solid witness testimony, even if it was second-hand. But the crew evidently wanted something much more visual, more of a definitively road-trip nature, which for the purposes of making the show interesting and visual for the viewers I totally understood, even if I didn't exactly agree with the approach taken. So, after a couple of hours of agitating the locals with the ear-splitting owl calls, and no doubt placing them in a state of high alert and terror in the process, we returned to the hotel, had a late supper, and said our goodnights.

The next day started normally. Mark drove me to the airport at Rochester, we shook hands, promised to keep in touch, and after clearing security I took my seat in the departure lounge and awaited my flight back home to Arlington, Texas. Little did I know it at the time, but this was the very same Rochester Airport where, only months earlier, a whole plane-load of passengers became infamously stranded, unable to leave the confines of the aircraft, and totally lacking in food and water for nearly a day. The reason: ridiculous bureaucratic bullshit in the "Age of Terror," what else?

When our plane was first delayed for an hour, then cancelled, then reinstated, then cancelled once more, and then *again* reinstated, word soon got around that we were in "*that* airport." Yes, we were. But, finally, we took to the air, amid claps, cheers, and sarcastic jokes, and by 10:00 p.m. I was sitting on the couch. Not for long, however: at around eight o'clock the following morning, I had to be back at Dallas-Fort Worth International Airport. I was due to fly to Albuquerque, New Mexico, where I was to rendezvous with my old mate, Greg Bishop, for a drive to an Angel Fire-based conference, at which we were both scheduled to lecture, Greg on UFOs and me on mysterious creatures. It was a gig that proved incredibly valuable in my pursuit of all things anomalistic and animalistic.

Chapter 5
The Monsters of Angel Fire

"Do *not* go down to the lake to see what it is!"

The Holographic Bigfoot

On landing at Albuquerque, I awaited the arrival of Greg Bishop who did not disappoint. Within 10 minutes of exiting the main doors, I was sitting in our rental car, fired up to hit the long road northwards. But as we were both famished and it was already 11:30 a.m., lunch was the absolute first order of the day. But this was destined to be no ordinary meal. It was a downright historic one.

Greg suggested that we telephone a local man, who he had come to know very well while researching and writing his UFO/conspiracy book of 2005, *Project Beta*, to join us. That man was Gabe Valdez, who unfortunately passed away in his sleep in August 2011. Back in the mid-to-late 1970s, when he held a position of standing within the New Mexico State Police, Gabe was heavily involved in the investigation of numerous, so-called "cattle mutilation" events in and around the New Mexican town of Dulce. It has long been rumored that below Dulce was a huge underground installation of the type that one would expect to see in a James Bond or Austin Powers movie; it was said to be controlled by a group of not exactly friendly extraterrestrials. [1]

So, we made our way to a Mexican restaurant that was one of Gabe's favorites, and we devoured our home-cooked nosh, sans frozen Margaritas, unfortunately. Gabe told some truly fascinating stories; others were undeniably surreal. More than once I nearly had to pinch myself as a reminder that the revelations coming our way were not those of a deranged fantasist or an over-the-top conspiracy theorist; they were being made by a former police officer who was highly respected.

Gabe told us that he was pretty sure there *was* a vast installation below Dulce, but whether it was inhabited and controlled by extraterrestrials, or by a secret arm of the U.S. military, was quite another matter entirely. He also opined that the cattle mutilation mystery was a very real one; however, he did not believe the curious killing and mutilation of animals all across the United States, especially those in the state of New Mexico, had anything *at all* to do with bug-eyed aliens from some far away galaxy. Rather, based upon the results of his own investigations and informed sources, Gabe had come to the thought-provoking conclusion that the UFO angle was nothing less than an ingenious cover story, one designed to mask what, in many ways, might be considered an even darker secret. That same secret revolved around a tale of covert elements of the military that were using the cattle in some type of clandestine germ warfare operation that was focused upon the development of new viruses for use as biological weapons.

Gabe also had a *very* odd story to tell about how he had come to believe that many New Mexico-based Bigfoot sightings were actually the work of a hidden arm of the U.S. Government that had the ability to create holograms of the hairy man-beasts. The purpose was to scare and deter local, superstitious people from getting too close to the government's underground installations. Again, to hear such a theory concerning Bigfoot coming out of the mouth of a respected police officer, and one who had been consulted by the FBI on matters of a cattle mutilation nature two decades earlier, was as profoundly amazing as it was truly unusual. Then with lunch over and Gabe's thought-provoking revelations on Bigfoot, cattle-mutilations and underground bases dissected and digested, it was time for Greg and I to head northwards to Angel Fire.

We made one other stop on the way: the Santa Fe veterans' cemetery, where a man named Paul Bennewitz was buried. Bennewitz's life, career, and UFO investigations, which so worried the U.S. Air Force in the late-1970s and early-1980s that they drove him nearly insane as they sought to bring his flying saucer studies to a halt, were the subject of Greg's book, *Project Beta*. On locating the cemetery, we drove in carefully, and finally located Bennewitz's grave. I set up my digital-recorder, while a visibly moved, and noticeably somber, Greg could not help but ponder upon how Bennewitz's passing was very likely hastened by the stress and anxiety generated by the Air Force's activities. Greg said, somewhat sadly: "I wish I could have told him 'thanks,' for having the story there to be written, and that I'm sorry he had to go through what he went through." [2]

Then, after a brief moment of silence, we really were bound for Angel Fire. The remainder of the journey was very cool with lots of winding roads, huge snow-capped peaks, the Rio Grande, and thick woods, all accompanied by CDs that varied from Devo to Los Punk Rockers and from Japanese punk to traditional New Mexican folk music. Angel Fire itself was also quite atmospheric. Although its population was barely a thousand, it was a very popular ski resort with a base elevation of 8,600 feet and a summit of nearly 11,000 feet and several kilometers of skiable terrain. [3]

We arrived about 4:00 p.m., checked in, showered, gulped down a couple of drinks at the bar, and then headed out to the meet and greet party, which had been arranged by the conference organizer, Janet Sailor. Just like conference organizers here, there, and everywhere, Janet was stressed and frazzled, which is precisely why I do not have any desire to ever plan and host a conference myself. But everything ultimately ran smoothly and on-time. [4] And as we sat and ate dinner with the rest of the speakers, which included UFO researchers Dennis Balthaser and Guy Malone, both of Roswell, and crashed UFO investigator Chuck Wade, I was most interested to learn that many of the attendees thought, as I did, that Bigfoot was very likely a paranormal entity, and not creature of flesh and blood. One of those was a local woman named Kristin Howard, whose story I will relate shortly.

Over the next two days, Greg and I delivered our lectures, hung out with the attendees, made the bar our second home, and generally had a good time as we listened to people relate their own weird experiences in Angel Fire. On the Saturday night, Greg and I headed into town and ate at a Mexican restaurant called *Tres Amigos*, where our waitress, overhearing us talking about the conference, asked if we were "scientists." We most certainly *aren't*, we told her! Not bothered by our lack of credentials, however, she told us of a number of Bigfoot sightings that had occurred in the area. Curiously, however, none of the creatures seen locally had exceeded five feet in height, and one of them was apparently carrying a large wooden club. In other words, Littlefoot was on the loose.

There was also the woman who came up to me on the second day of the gig to relate how she had seen a giant beast, resembling a pterodactyl, flying above a road just outside of town a couple of years earlier, and which eerily echoed the 2006 event at Wisconsin that indirectly led to my appearance on *MonsterQuest's* Mothman episode in 2009. But, without doubt it was the story of a local woman, Kristin Howard, that fascinated me most, and which unraveled in truly sensational style in the weeks that immediately followed the conference and my trip back to Texas.

A Witness Speaks

I sat and ate dinner with Kristin and several other conference attendees on the first night of the gig. She proceeded to tell me some fascinating stories about Bigfoot and expressed her opinion that the species might be a sort of caretaker of nature. We developed a good rapport and promised to stay in touch. Approximately 2:00 a.m. on September 28, I received an email from Kristin who wanted to share with me something that had just happened on her property. It turned out that around 11:00 p.m. (New Mexico time) the night before, Kristin was about to enter her apartment when she "heard something unusual" coming from within the lake where she and her mother live. Whatever it was, it didn't sound like a normal animal. Kristin noted to me: "The sound was rhythmic, like large, regular strokes were being taken. Likewise, because of the regular long strokes, I also dismissed the possibility of it being a bear."

Kristin quickly returned to her mother's place—their homes are connected to each other—and asked if she had heard anything unusual. The response of Kristin's mother's was forthright and to the point: "Go back to your apartment and close the door and lock it, and whatever you do, don't go wandering around outside in the dark and do *not* go down to the lake to see what it is!" Given that the loud sounds suggested something very big and powerful swimming the lake by night, and the fact that Kristin told me "folks speak of sightings in this area," she began to wonder if a Bigfoot was on the loose.

I found Kristin's account to be of deep and overriding interest, and offered her both my thoughts and a few pieces of advice. And it wouldn't be long before there was a new development in the story. On September 30, Kristin told me that the previous evening she had been walking her dog when she suddenly heard "what sounded like a high-pitched electronic whine from a distance." And it coincided with the local coyote population going into an absolute frenzy of howling. But that was only the beginning of the night's events.

At around 11:15, just before retiring for the night, Kristin headed down her balcony steps to her car to retrieve a parcel containing a new pack of tarot cards. As she did so, the same, curious, high-pitched whine could be heard. This time, however, it was much closer: perhaps no more than 20 feet away. And it was immediately followed by what Kristin described as "a rather aggressive growl." She admitted to me: "It wasn't until I was back safely in my apartment that I started to shake; the growl hadn't been ferocious, but it was definitely intimidating, and even perhaps a bit threatening."

Nine days later, there came yet another email from Kristin: "I think I figured out the growl; earlier that day I had made a tea with several different herbs, including rosehips, and had put the plant material outside. The growl had come from near where I'd left the plant material; the next day I checked and sure enough, the plant material had been disturbed. It appeared to be methodically 'pawed' in a single direction and a straight line, rather than strewn about haphazardly as a bear or dog or other critter might do. So, my guess is that, whatever it was, it was busy pawing through the plant material (in search of the rosehips, perhaps) when I surprised it, and it did that strange electronic-sounding whine and growled to alert me to its presence."

October 16 brought forth another email. Several nights earlier, Kristin was walking her dog when she heard "a big bunch of crashing, like several tree-limbs breaking at once." Bigfoot? Maybe. Kristin added, however, that word was afoot in the area that a mountain lion had been seen locally. A connection perhaps?

Almost a month later Kristin wrote again: "I heard one pretty clearly the other night through my open window…At first I thought it was a dog barking, and then an owl hooting. It wasn't until I went to the window and listened closely that I could tell it wasn't anything of the sort. I heard ape-like hoots, as well as a very 'human' questioning sort of 'hoot.' The hoot repeated again, so I went to get my tape recorder and tiptoed outside, but the creature got quiet."

While Kristin was certainly on a quest for evidence, she did not wish to disturb the Bigfoot that she believed was possibly lurking nearby: "They're obviously pretty private beings and I have no desire to open them up to exposure…quite the contrary." Her closing words: "At this point, I'm starting to think that perhaps they came because of my wish for an ally and so now they're here, and we're both like, 'Now what…?'"

Now what, indeed? I've kept in touch with Kristin, but events seemed to trail-off. But, should matters one day again escalate, I told Kristin, I will once again be Angel Fire-bound and hot on the trail of the mystery beast. [5]

Celebrating the Creature of the Lake

Only a few weeks after the Angel Fire, New Mexico gig, I attended the first of a now-ongoing series of events celebrating the legend of a strange monster seen decades ago, and only a short distance from where I live. Back in the summer of 1969, something exceedingly strange happened at Lake Worth, Texas. As the witnesses told it, a wild, bipedal creature with horns, cloven hooves, and "scale"-like skin was seen on several occasions roaming the woods and roads of the lake, striking terror into those who crossed its path. Witnesses reported seeing a big, fast-moving beast that jumped on their cars and flung a large tire at a group of people who were in the area trying to find the creature. The cops carefully scoured the woods for any evidence of the thing, and the local media was highly entertained in the process. And thus was born the legend of the Goat Man. [6]

Since then, the tales of the Goat Man have become infamous in and around Lake Worth. The legend has as many disbelievers as it does supporters. For some, mistaken identity, hoaxing, and hysteria can explain just about everything. Others have concluded that Bigfoot was to blame, while there are those, like me, who find the whole story very intriguing but who have not formed any strong opinion one way or the other, mainly as a result of the inevitable passage of time and a lack of hard evidence one way or the other.

The Goat Man has been the subject of a full-length book (*The Lake Worth Monster* by Sallie Ann Clarke), a couple of TV documentaries, numerous newspaper stories, and even a song or two. [7] And that's not all. Saturday, October 3, 2009, saw the first ever "Lake Worth Monster Bash" held at the lake, right in the heart of Goat Man Territory, or as it's known today, the Fort Worth Nature Center and Refuge. [8]

I have to confess that when I set off for the lake around 9:00 a.m. that morning, I wondered if anyone would actually show up. After all, how many people would want to learn about the 40-year-old story of a beast described as being half-man and half-goat? Actually, the answer was: quite a lot. By around 11:00 a.m., the parking lot was practically full, and the crowds were out in force. And there was much to do and see, too. Recognizing that the Goat Man was, and still is, an integral part of Lake Worth's history, the FWNCR put on a great event. Craig Woolheater and the Texas Bigfoot Research Conservancy were there, highlighting the work of the group. And Sean Whitley, the writer, director and co-producer of *Southern Fried Bigfoot*, an excellent documentary on Bigfoot in the American South, had a table promoting his film. [9]

For those who wanted to get into the spirit of the Goat Man legend, there was the "Throw like the Pro–Tire Hurling Contest," where people could try and recreate the Goat Man's legendary tire-throwing caper of 1969. There was a hike to Greer Island, a small body on the lake where the beast has supposedly been seen on a number of occasions, and a trip to the quarry where the tire-tossing incident occurred. And for the children, there was a reading of the book *Cam the Man Hunts for the Spooky Goat Man*, written by local author Stephanie Erb, and a chance for them to build their own creepy creature at the Kids' Monster Headquarters. [10]

In addition, there were some very welcome stalls and displays that highlighted local wildlife, including exotic insects and much more. And there was music on-hand, too: the *Skip Pullig Band* played their new song, titled "The Goat Man." Well, what else *could* it have been titled? And things didn't end there. [11]

Sallie Ann Clarke had loaned her priceless collection of Goat Man memorabilia to Lake Worth's Hardwicke Visitor's Center, which now has a whole section devoted to his Royal Goatness. Plus canoe tours around Greer Island, a chance to feed the island's resident population of Bison, and hayrides around the lake were all part and parcel of the day's events. Put simply, this was very much a fun, family-oriented, interactive experience that paid homage to the original legend of the Goat Man, but one that also allowed people to learn about the important work of the FWNCR. And it got the kids away from the computers and the TVs for a while, and let them see that there is a real world outside, full of fresh air—and weirdness.

But, perhaps most important of all, the event prompted those who had seen the beast for themselves to relate their accounts to interested parties. One of those was Mack Barlow, who I met at the Bash, and who told me three days later in an in-depth interview that he had seen the Goat Man on a Saturday night in March 2009. The location wasn't the lake itself, but a road running adjacent to the lake, Barlow explained. He said it was around 11:00 p.m., and he had been driving home after attending a wedding, when he caught sight of an odd, man-like form standing at the side of the road "where there was a bunch of trees behind."

The creature, Barlow added, was around seven feet tall and "man-shaped." But, this was no normal man. The entity sported two horny, goat-like protrusions from its head. Its lower body was covered entirely in fur. It wasn't a local, in other words. Barlow, of course, knew of the 1960s stories of the Goat Man, and so he floored the accelerator, preferring not to become the creature's next meal. Quite reasonably, I asked Barlow if it was possible that he had merely been the victim of a good-natured hoax. He didn't outright deny that as a possibility, but said: "The Goat Man is real and I saw him. People can say what they want, but I saw him." [12]

And Barlow wasn't alone.

A second, hitherto unknown, story that surfaced at the Goat Man gig came from an elderly woman named Marlene Devorss, who had the misfortune to have a run-in with the beast back in 1978. A resident of the city of Fort Worth at the time, Devorss, like Mack Barlow, had her encounter while visiting the town of Lake Worth. As we sat and chatted, Devorss told me she had seen what she described as a "huge, just huge!" bipedal animal race across a stretch of road near the lake, at around 9:00 or 10:00 p.m. on a weekday night. Notably, it sported a massive pair of horns, *the* calling card of the Goat Man. And its fur was utterly white in color, she said.

I knew that sightings of white Bigfoot do surface from time to time. Doing my very best not to influence her next response, I asked Devorss if it was possible she had seen a Bigfoot, rather than a Goat Man. Devorss was certain she had not seen Bigfoot: "I don't know much about these things, but Bigfoot doesn't have horns, does he?" She had a good point. I conceded that, no, Bigfoot most certainly does *not* sport a pair of horns.

"So, I saw the Goat Man," she said, more than slightly defensively, and with her arms folded tight across her middle.

Who was I to argue? [13]

Chapter 6
Sacrificed Frogs and
Stone-Faced Werewolves

"I found a small frog with its legs broken slowly dying in a cold stream."

Space-Brother Synchronicities
Undoubtedly one of the strangest and most unsettling aspects of any paranormal investigation occurs when the phenomenon itself decides to suddenly turn the tables and takes on the investigator, himself or herself. This has occurred to me on several memorable occasions, but never to the sheer and graphic extent it did in 2009, while I was researching the so-called Contactee movement. My research was at its height when a truly bizarre set of synchronistic and near-unearthly events occurred that had me questioning both my sanity and grip on reality. That they spilled over into a strange animal-connected story was, well, even stranger!

George Adamski, Truman Bethurum, Billy Meier, and Daniel Fry were just a few of those curious souls who, many decades ago, claimed face-to-face interaction with long-haired, human-looking alien entities who wanted our nuclear arsenals disarmed and peace and harmony for mankind. The era of the Contactee was, to say the least, one of the most unusual within what has become known popularly as UFOlogy. That high-strangeness became very personal for me in July 2009. [1]

At the time, I was studying the life and UFO experiences of a 1950s contactee named Dana Howard, who claimed a number of meetings and exchanges with a beautiful, eight-foot-tall Venusian named Diana, several of which occurred during séances held at a Los Angeles-based church. An Oregon-based researcher and writer named Regan Lee, who had spent a great deal of time investigating the claims of Dana Howard, had provided me with information on her case. [2]

On July 31, I wrote an email to Regan immediately after

digesting the data she sent me on the Dana Howard affair: "...I took some towels out of the dryer. One of the towels [was] a yellow and pink one. But for all the time [I] have had the towel, I never bothered to read the writing on it—until I was folding the towel right after finishing your chapter." [3]

As I told Regan, the towel was adorned with a logo that read: *Venus Girls Just Want to Have Fun*. Well, it must have been just some weird coincidence, right? As I was to find out later on, there was something far stranger than mere coincidence at work. [4]

Frogs and Folklore
On the night of November 30, 2009, I was interviewed on a radio show about the Contactee movement, and I commented that there had been a number of encounters with the longhaired, so-called Space Brothers in the vicinity of England's famous Stonehenge. Well, it so happens that, in 2008, I actually built my very own recreation of Stonehenge in my backyard, a smaller version of it, of course. Yes, I know it's weird, and I guess it's fair to say that I am, too!

So imagine my surprise when, two days after the show aired, I was out in the yard cleaning some fallen leaves off of my fish-pond, when I saw, atop one of my Stonehenge stones, a frog. It was very dead and quite shrivelled. The odd positioning of the frog provoked in my mind disturbing imagery of some strange ritualistic sacrifice having been undertaken in the yard during the dead of night, by forces unknown, and while I blissfully slept. The frog-themed weirdness didn't end there, however.

When I made a brief mention of this curious event on one of my many blogs, a correspondent posted the following to the "Comments" section: "For your amusement and mystification, a small section from the footnotes of Jason Louv's *A Grammary in Ultraculture, Journal One* bears directly on the sacrifice of frogs: 'When I was twelve I was sent to camp for a week on Mount Palomar, as the San Diego public school system did to all sixth-graders at this time. At one point I found a small frog with its legs broken, slowly dying in a cold stream. Feeling horrible for the frog, I put it in a plastic bag and showed it to a camp counsellor. At this age I had an aquarium with two bull-frogs in it in my room who I regularly fed and cared for, I told the camp counsellor that I wanted to bring the frog home and nurse it back to health. The counsellor decided to take it upon himself to teach me a lesson about *the way things really are* and made me put it back in the stream to die, *as is the course of nature.* This began to compound my already growing hatred of authority figures. When I went home, already heartbroken, I found that in my absence one of my own pet frogs had gotten itself smashed in between a large rock and the edge of the aquarium and gutted itself (a pet snake had also died). Later, when I was seventeen, I bought a copy of *Paranoia* magazine with an article about Jack Parsons in it, which included the rather stunning factoid that Jack Parsons and the Agape Lodge of the O.T.O. had crucified a frog on Mount Palomar in the Forties.'" [5]

I found this was highly interesting for several reasons, one being that Mount Palomar is situated in San Diego County, California, and it is where, back in 1944, George Adamski, arguably the ultimate contactee, purchased 20-acres of land with the financial help of several friends. The group subsequently constructed a new home for themselves, called Palomar Gardens, and opened a restaurant, the Palomar Gardens Cafe. It wasn't long before something otherworldly and significant put in an appearance. On October 9, 1946, Adamski and a number of his friends claimed that while they were at the Palomar Gardens' campground, they saw a huge cigar-shaped UFO shoot across the sky. Then, one year later, Adamski photographed what appeared to be the very same gigantic craft, once again at Palomar Gardens. [6]

As for Jack Parsons, he was a noted occultist and a near-genius in the field of rocketry, who in the late 1930s fell under the spell of the "Great Beast" himself, Aleister Crowley, who had also engaged in a rite involving the sacrifice of a frog in 1916 at the New Hampshire cottage of an astrologer named Evangeline Adams. Despite his initial objections to sacrificing a living animal, Crowley resolved to crucify the frog (his "willing familiar," as he later referred to the unfortunate animal) "with the idea ... that some supreme violation of all the laws of my being would break down my Karma or dissolve the spell that seems to bind me." The sacrifice was intended to assist in Crowley's development as an occultist, which is precisely what encouraged Jack Parsons to follow a similar sacrificial path at Mount Palomar. [7]

I elected to look a little deeper into the strange world of the frog, a creature that has a long and checkered history when it comes to mythology, folklore, superstition, and the occult. In medieval Europe, the frog was seen as a creature of the Devil, as the Catholic Church had identified the frog as a witch's familiar, a familiar being a creature that serves its witch-master and that may bewitch the enemies of its owner. As far as the ancient Egyptians were concerned, the frog was perceived as a symbol of life and fertility, since millions of them were born after the annual inundation of the Nile, which brought fertility to the otherwise barren lands. Consequently, in Egyptian mythology, there emerged nothing less than a frog goddess, named Heget, who represented fertility. Likewise, the Greeks and Romans also associated frogs with fertility and harmony. Moving on to China, the frog was linked with healing and good fortune in business. And this was also echoed in bonny Scotland, where, in centuries past, the frog was seen as being a creature of welcoming good luck. [8]

So here I was, researching George Adamski and his experiences at Mount Palomar, which happened to be precisely where Aleister Crowley's disciple Jack Parsons was sacrificing frogs in the late 1940s, and who was following in the path of his diabolical mentor who had done something very similar in 1916. And the culmination of all this was the discovery at the same time of what looked like a sacrificed frog on my very own mini-Stonehenge! On top of that, during the same period all this weirdness was taking place, I was deeply involved in the writing of my book *Final Events*, substantial chapters of which were focused on the lives and activities of...Jack Parsons and Aleister Crowley! [9]

Spies from the Skies
If a dead, sacrificed frog sitting on a mini Stonehenge wasn't enough to deal with, my house at this time began receiving both daylight and nighttime visits by military helicopters. Such craft—"phantom helicopters" or "black helicopters," as they are known to UFO researchers—often appear, quite out of the blue, in situations where UFO-related activity has taken place. Some investigators believe the helicopters are piloted by personnel attached to an elite and secret group within the American military, whose job it is to keep a careful and clandestine watch on those exposed to the UFO phenomenon and those who dared to investigate its complexities. Based on what

happened, I was hardly in a position to argue with that theory. [10]

One such helicopter, a Chinook, rumbled over my home late one night and briefly lit up the backyard with a powerful and brilliant spotlight. Others were far more brazen, appearing in daylight, and practically posing for me as I shot photograph after photograph as they circled directly overhead. "You're on to something and they're trying to intimidate you," one colleague suggested. [11]

And still the lack of normalcy persisted.

Two days after I appeared on the radio show talking about longhaired brothers from outer space, I was sitting on the couch, reading the newly-surfaced account of a person who in the 1970s had a Contactee-style experience that in many ways paralleled the 1952 encounters of Truman Bethurum, whose claims I related in my *Contactees* book of 2009. According to Bethurum, on a number of occasions at a place called Mormon Mesa, Nevada, he met with a group of aliens led by their Captain, the very hot and shapely Aura Rhanes, who came from a planet supposedly called Clarion. Of course, like most of the stories of the contactees, Bethurum's was highly controversial and it attracted just about as many disbelievers as it did believers. Although I am of the opinion that Bethurum had an interaction with *something*, just what that something was is a matter of debate and personal interpretation. [12]

Anyway, after I put away the file on this newly-surfaced story, which very much reminded me of Bethurum's experiences with a certain curvy Clarionite, I was on the hunt for a digital camera that had been misplaced somewhere in the house. I looked high and low, but failed to locate it. But, while checking behind the TV set to see if the camera had perhaps fallen there, I came across an old high-school yearbook for 1982. What on earth does all this have to do with the contactees? I'm coming to that.

The cover of the book read: *82 Clarion*. Of course, skeptically-minded souls might say this was all some bizarre coincidence. I did, however, find it odd that after spending about two hours reading a report very similar to that of Truman Bethurum and his friends from Clarion, that I should immediately afterwards stumble across a book with that very word Clarion adorned across its front cover.

In view of all this, perhaps I can be forgiven for thinking that each and every one us live in a dream world of truly *Matrix* proportions!

And I have one more story to share with you of how digging into Fortean phenomena can lead the researcher into distinctly strange pathways. This one, however, is saturated with outright paranormal hostility, in my view at least. And, as you'll see, I should know...

That Hellish Head

Paradise is a small Texan town, situated about a 30-minute drive from the sprawling city of Fort Worth. It's dominated by isolated homes, thick woods, sprawling fields, numerous cows, and very little else. Aside, that is, from a killer-werewolf. Dawn had just broken one day in September 1996, when Walter, a rancher who then made Paradise his home, headed out to tend his cows, which had the run of a large field at the back of his property. Walter was not expecting to find the horrifying scene upon which he stumbled. One of his most valuable cows had been killed under cover of darkness. And, by the looks of the cow, the killer had been some sort of vicious, powerful creature that surely had no place prowling the fields of Paradise. The cow was disemboweled, its throat ripped out, and both back legs were missing.

Although Walter wasted no time in contacting the police, this turned out to be an utterly fruitless task, since the only thing the responding officers could suggest to the irate and worried rancher was that perhaps a big cat was responsible and was still on the loose. And while this was certainly a major cause for alarm and a matter they would most definitely look into, it was not, technically speaking, a crime that required the attention of the police. That's right, the cops were far too busy dishing out tickets to people who dared drive one mile per hour over the speed limit.

So a wholly dissatisfied and disgusted Walter decided to take matters into his own hands and embarked upon a series of night-time vigils in the hope that the beast might return and that he, Walter, would have the opportunity to blow the creature's head clean off its shoulders, and put an end to the matter before it risked spiraling wildly out of control.

Thus it was that at roughly 2:00 a.m. four days later, while dutifully scanning the field with a nightscope that was attached to his high-powered gun, Walter became frozen with fear when he caught sight of a large, hairy figure striding across the field. Around seven feet in height, very muscular and dark, it had the body of a man, but the face, the ears and the muzzle of what looked like a large German shepherd dog or a wild wolf. Rooted to the spot, Walter didn't even think to fire his gun. Rather, he simply watched, dumbstruck with fear, as the beast covered the width of the field very quickly, and vanished into the trees that bordered his property.

Rather ominously, only a short time later and in the same exact spot where he first noticed the diabolical wolf-man, Walter found in the grass a small, stone, carved head of a fanged monster with slits for eyes and flared nostrils. Walter quickly became convinced that occultists had been secretly at work his field, engaged in some unholy act, and had quite literally invoked the hair-covered beast from another realm of existence.

When Walter related the extraordinary tale to me, high up on his list of priorities was to finally get rid of the unsettling carved head, which he had stored in his garage, fearful of having it in the house, or even of dumping it himself and risk facing some sort of beastly backlash. Actually, being done with the skull wasn't just high on Walter's list, it was at the absolute top of it. Well, as someone whose office shelves are home to the skull of a coyote (or of a Texas Chupacabras—take your pick), the preserved remains of a large stingray, a piece of brickwork from the Mothman-haunted TNT plant at Point Pleasant, West Virginia, and even an old rusted pistol that I found on the shore of a stretch of Texan beach in the summer of 2003, I said to Walter something like, "How about I take the head off your hands?" A mightily relieved Walter was more than happy to hand the head over to me, and I was pleased to place it right next to my stingray. [13]

A Belly-Full of Problems

After a few days, I came to realize there was something very odd and unsettling about that stone head of Walter's. When it was held up to the light, or placed in a shadowy environment, its appearance seemed to change slightly, sometimes to a maniacal glare, and occasionally to what resembled a cruel, cold sneer. There's absolutely no doubt that it *was* all just due to tricks of the light and the shadows; the head, I need to stress, was *not* literally changing its form. But the fact that shadows caused the face to take on such specifically gruesome appearances seemed beyond chance. It was almost as if someone had ingeniously, skillfully, and deliberately, fashioned the head in such a way that its appearance would *seem* to change, radically so even, and not once in a welcoming fashion.

I hardly ever touched the head in the years it was in my possession, as it actually did disturb me, but for reasons I could never really understand. Late one night in January 2010, however, I was lying on my living room couch, with the head in my left hand and my digital camera in my right hand. It was my intention to photograph the head with my fingers in the picture for scale, so that people would have an idea of the size of the head, and then post the picture to my cryptozoology-themed blog, *There's Something in the Woods*, along with the background details of Walter's eerie encounter. It had been a long day and night, however, and I fell fast asleep before I was able to do so.

I was roused from my slumber around 3:00 a.m. by thunder booming and lightning flashing, with the camera on the couch, and the head resting squarely on my stomach, face up. Its malevolent sneer was illuminated up by the light of a nearby table lamp. I groggily tossed everything, including the head, to one side and went to bed. The next morning I woke up with a horrible stomach ache. Later that night I began passing blood and mucus. There followed a terrifying two weeks filled with thoughts of some dread terminal disease. It transpired that I had been hit by a spectacular case of *E. coli*.

Was it only a coincidence that the problem began immediately after the accursed head sat atop my stomach, sneering at me as I awoke from my deep sleep the very night before? You may think I am being downright crazy, but I wasted no time at all in throwing the head into a bag, and placing it outside for the garbage collectors to take away. Since that very day, and as someone who rarely ever gets sick, my stomach has been problem-free. There's practically nothing in the realms of the cryptozoological, paranormal, supernatural, or ufological that unsettles or intimidates me. But Walter's stone head, I freely admit, succeeded in doing both.

Chapter 7
The Curious Caper of the Cardiff Giant

"A most decided humbug…"

Gigging with the Ghost Hunters

Friday, January 8, 2010, was a monumentally cold one in Dallas, Texas, and as I boarded my morning flight to Albany, New York, I guessed it was going to get even colder. Wrong, I most definitely was not. After a several hours long layover in chilly Chicago, I arrived at snow blanketed Albany International Airport around 4:00 p.m. I made my way to baggage-claim and sat and awaited a shuttle to the Ghosts of Cooperstown gig, where I was due to lecture on my expeditions in search of the Puerto Rican Chupacabras, British werewolves, Scottish lake-monsters, and Texan Goat Men. The conference was the brainchild of the SyFy Channel's *Ghost Hunters* crew; it was the second such event of theirs at which I had spoken. [1]

At the first such gig some nine months earlier at New Hampshire's Mount Washington Hotel, a host of good stories regarding beastly entities came my way, and I hoped this occasion would prove to be equally profitable. It most certainly did. By the time our driver arrived around 5:30 p.m., the steady but unspectacular snowfall that was in evidence 90-minutes earlier now looked like the dawning of a new Ice Age. The seven of us who were scheduled to take the ride pulled our collars high and our hoods low, exited baggage-claim, and made our way through the growing blizzard to the snow-blanketed parking lot.

I assumed we were being driven to the gig by SuperShuttle or some similar outfit, but the *Ghost Hunters* gang had arranged for us to be picked up by a cop from Cooperstown who had a personal interest in the paranormal. With him behind the wheel, skillfully negotiating the treacherous roads at breakneck speed, the journey began.

At one point, as we neared our final destination, a large deer ran out into the road, only narrowly managing to avoid being turned into a tasty pile of venison. As it did so, someone in the back of the van remarked, only jokingly, that they thought for an instant the animal was nothing less than Bigfoot. Well, it was that aside which led our cop friend to relate a few stories that had come his way in Cooperstown over the years. We all listened intently as the snow continued to pour, visibility lessened dramatically, and the skies grew ever darker and bleaker, much to my strange satisfaction.

One story concerned the unusual deaths in the area some three of four years earlier of numerous deer, all of which displayed clear evidence of savage bite marks to their necks. Were vampires on the loose? Was a Chupacabras rampaging around the woods of Cooperstown? Not according to the official story that our driver told us. Coyotes were the culprits, wildlife officials had suggested. He added that this did not, however, put to rest the rumors that a savage black cat of impressive size was roaming around the area. And that wasn't his only big cat story.

Our driver confided in us how he was personally aware of a case that had occurred around the same time as the deer killings, when a woman in the area of Cooperstown had shot and killed a mountain lion that had been invading her property with disturbing regularity. She had then stuffed the corpse into the trunk of her car and headed to the offices of the same wildlife officials who had attempted to put to rest the stories that vampires were feeding on the town's deer population. Then, so the tale went, a Fox Mulder-worthy cover-up began in earnest. The following morning, the woman returned to the offices of the wildlife people and asked what they were going to do about the mountain lion presence in the area. She logically reasoned that if there was one large, predatory cat prowling around, then there might very well be another, and another and...

The terse response to the woman's questions was: "What mountain lion?"

"The dead one I brought to your offices yesterday!" she boomed, both angry and astonished. The wildlife personnel claimed no knowledge at all of any such corpse, until the woman pulled out of her jacket-pocket various photos of the animal, taken in the trunk of her vehicle, with the wildlife offices in the background. Possibly anticipating that the authorities might want to downplay, or even deny, that large cats were on the loose in the vicinity, the woman had the very good presence of mind to capture the evidence for posterity.

Faced with the undeniable proof, the wildlife officer radically changed his approach. He apologized to the extent that most government officials are able and asked the woman not to talk about the affair, largely as a result of the probably correct worry that the local media would sensationalize the entire matter, and countless people would then be running around the woods at night, shooting just anything that moved, including quite possibly each other. Of course, this tale possessed more than a few aspects of Men in Black lore: the government official, the missing evidence, and the veiled warning not to discuss the issue. That the story was coming from a serving police officer, however, made it all the more thought-provoking to those of us listening carefully in the cold van.

It was on the Saturday night of the *Ghost Hunters* gig, however, when a definitively surreal air overcame the event. While hanging out in the bar around 8:00 p.m., a fragmentary (*very* fragmentary, it must be admitted) story reached my ears from a man who had then recently returned from serving with the military in the Middle East. He had heard tales of large, marauding werewolves roaming by night the mountains of Afghanistan and some of the more ancient parts of Iraq. The U.S. Army secretly knew all about the beasts, I was earnestly told, but didn't know how to handle the situation, and even lacked any real understanding of what the creatures were or from where, exactly, they came. And so the military simply chose to take the easiest of all approaches available: they outright ignored the reports, or wrote them off as the equivalent of campfire tales told to kids on Halloween.

"Is there any way I can get this validated?" I asked the man.

"Nope," he replied, in a matter-of-fact fashion, as we drank our double whiskies. "But it *is* true, every bit of it."

The Cardiff Creature Caper

The sensational tale of the legendary Cardiff Giant is just about as weird, as surreal, and as convoluted as any tale can possibly get. It is also one of the most infamous and audacious hoaxes in American history, one with an integral tie to Cooperstown. Essentially, the giant was said to be a 10-foot-tall "petrified man," uncovered on October 16, 1869, by workmen engaged in digging a well behind the barn belonging to William C. "Stub" Newell in Cardiff, New York. In reality, however, the giant was nothing of the sort. It was actually the creation of a New York tobacconist named George Hull. He was an atheist who decided to create the mighty form after a heated argument with a fundamentalist minister, a Mr. Turk, about the passage in Genesis 6:4 to the effect that giants once roamed the Earth.

Hull secretly hired a group of men to carve the enormous figure out of a block of gypsum in Fort Dodge, Iowa, telling them it was to be used in the creation of a monument to Abraham Lincoln that would stand proudly in New York City. But that was just about as far away from the truth as it was possible to get. When the work was complete, Hull secretly shipped the block to Chicago, where he hired a German stonecutter to further carve it into the likeness of a man, not forgetting, in the process, to swear him to absolute secrecy.

The ruse was ingenious and required a great deal of careful and dedicated work. A variety of stains and acids were used to make the giant appear both ancient and weathered. In addition, the giant's surface was beaten with steel knitting needles embedded in a board. The purpose? To simulate pores on the skin. If nothing else, Hull had skillfully thought out his grand scheme. Then, in November 1868, Hull transported the giant by rail to the farm of his cousin, a man named William Newell. No less than $2,600 was spent on the hoax in total, which was a sizeable amount of money back in the 1860s.

Almost 12 months later, Newell hired Gideon Emmons and Henry Nichols, ostensibly to dig a well, and on October 16, 1869, lo and behold the pair "found" the Cardiff Giant. One of the men reportedly exclaimed, in excited and exaggerated tones guaranteed to be overheard by people in the immediate area: "I declare: some old Indian has been buried here!" But that was only the start of the matter. Newell quickly set up a tent over the giant and charged 25 cents each time anyone wanted to see it. Two days later, very pleased by the huge number of people who turned out to view the Cardiff Giant, Newell increased the price to 50 cents. Enterprise truly was the name of this game.

Archaeological scholars quickly pronounced the giant as being a fake, while a number of geologists noticed there was no logical reason for digging a well in the exact spot in which the giant had been found. Yale paleontologist Othniel C. Marsh came right to the point, famously declaring the Cardiff Giant "a most decided humbug." There were, however, some gullible Christian fundamentalists and preachers who defended its legitimacy. Ultimately, Hull sold his part-interest for the very impressive sum of $37,500 to a syndicate of five men headed by one David Hannum. They then clandestinely moved the giant form to Syracuse, New York, for exhibition. Unsurprisingly, the giant drew such massive crowds that the famous showman P.T. Barnum offered a stunning $60,000 for a three-month lease of the giant. When the syndicate flatly turned him down, the always resourceful and industrious Barnum hired a man to create a plaster replica, which quickly went on display in New York amid claims that this was the real thing, and that the Cardiff Giant was the hoax!

As newspaper journalists gleefully reported on Barnum's version of the story, David Hannum was quoted as saying, "There's a sucker born every minute," in reference to spectators paying to see Barnum's giant. Over time, the quotation was misattributed to P.T. Barnum, himself, and still is to this day. Hannum then tried to sue Barnum. The judge, who had a good sense of humor, told Hannum to get his giant to swear on his own genuineness in court if he wanted an injunction in his favor. But still matters were not over. On December 10, Hull confessed the truth to the press. Then, two months later, on February 2, 1870, both giants were revealed as fakes in court, and the judge ruled that Barnum could not be sued for calling a fake giant a fake. And that was the end of the bizarre lawsuit.

But the events encouraged others to come forward with their very own versions of the Cardiff Giant. In 1876, the "Solid Muldoon" surfaced out of Beulah, Colorado, and was exhibited at 50 cents a ticket. There was also a rumor going around that Barnum had offered to buy it for $20,000. It was, needless to say, another fake, and possibly one in which George Hull himself had a hand.

One year later, in 1877, the owner of Taughannock House hotel on Cayuga Lake, New York, hired his own dedicated band of men to create a large, petrified man, carefully placing it precisely where the workers who were expanding the hotel would eventually find it. Once again, media-based publicity and public interest were most impressive.

Then in 1892, a certain Jefferson "Soapy" Smith, of the town of Creede, Colorado, bought a petrified man—"McGinty," as he became known—for $3,000 and exhibited the body for 10 cents a look. Interestingly, this giant was actually a real one. It was a human body that had been deliberately injected with chemicals used for preservation. Soapy enthusiastically displayed McGinty from 1892 to 1895 throughout Colorado and the northwest United States. Seven years on, a petrified man was supposedly found in Fort Benton, Montana. The body was supposedly identified as that of a U.S. Civil War general named Thomas Francis Meagher. Meagher had drowned in the Missouri River two years previously. The petrified man was transported to New York for exhibition, but, needless to say, it was not the general, at all.

The Cardiff Giant, which had started the fuss, continued to surface from time to time, but its place in the limelight was clearly waning. In 1901 the giant appeared on display at the Pan-American Exposition but failed to generate any significant attention or publicity. Then, some years later, an Iowa-based publisher purchased it for use as a coffee table! Eventually growing tired of the giant, the man sold it in 1947 to the Farmers' Museum in Cooperstown, New York, only a few short minutes' drive from the very hotel at which, in January 2010, I was lecturing for the *Ghost Hunters*. [2]

A Goliath of the Forest

After hearing the engaging story of the werewolves of the Middle East, a Cooperstown-based, 20-something woman who I'll call "Sarah" came up to me in the bar, sat down with a margarita in hand, and swore to me that her father had seen the Cardiff Giant striding through the woods of Cooperstown late one winter's night in 2007. I asked Sarah if she, or her father, were joking. She assured me they most certainly were not. Sarah's father, she said, had been driving home at around 11:00 p.m. one Friday night, after visiting friends in Albany. As Sarah's father approached a stretch of road enveloped by trees, he was shocked by the sight of the Cardiff Giant looming out of the woods, striding across the road in several massive steps, and into the trees on the other side of the road.

Not surprisingly, he hit the brakes hard and could only watch in amazement and awe as the Goliath-like form lumbered into the darkened trees. Sarah told me both she and her father, both locals, had been to see the Cardiff Giant on display at the local museum on several occasions over the years. They also knew full well that it was nothing more than a century-plus old hoax. So how could a hoaxed creation be seen wandering the chilled woods of Cooperstown in 2007? Well, it couldn't, under any circumstances. That does not mean the case was without merit, however.

Sarah's opinion was that the Cardiff Giant her father saw was most certainly not the same entity that currently rests in the Farmer's Museum. Rather, she felt, he had been blessed with a sighting of a thought-form—a tulpa—that had been conjured into existence unconsciously by those who had seen the exhibit at the museum and who earnestly wished to accept the giant was real. It was a mind-monster, in other words, one that cannot exist and thrive unless people believe in it. It was as good a theory as any. And, as readers of my previous books will be acutely aware, the phenomenon of the tulpa is one that intrigues me.

Sarah asked me: "Would you like to check out the woods with me tonight and see if we can find the giant?" Why not? It was after midnight when a bunch of us finally headed out to the woods. It turns out that someone had overheard our conversation at the bar, and I was soon inundated by a mass of people all wanting to come along on the gigantic quest.

Ultimately, as the weather worsened and the temperature plummeted, only seven of us braved the harsh weather and the wild woods, armed with cameras and audio-equipment. By 1:00 a.m., the temperature was way below zero, and I do not exaggerate when I say that if we had not dressed to the nines in thick clothing, we would likely have been hauled out of those woods in body bags! Despite the fact that we hung out until around 3:00 a.m. where Sarah's father had encountered the lumbering form back in 2007, and even though we tried to invoke the goliath-sized form for ourselves, nothing wicked our way came that night. We returned to the hotel foyer, cold, clammy, and hungry. The Cardiff Giant, in tulpa form, remained elusive.

Chapter 8
Shape-Shifters and Creepy Camels

"It's started; they're coming."

The Birds by the Doors

The first half of 2010 was overshadowed by my mother's increasingly poor and fragile health. She had been diagnosed with Alzheimer's while still in her late fifties, some 14 years earlier. And taking into consideration the nightmarish situation that inevitably befalls the Alzheimer's sufferer, her tragic, but not unexpected, passing in June 2010 was in some ways as much a blessing as it was a huge shock for me and—after 55 years of happy, loving marriage—for my dad, Frank. But, we coped as best as anyone copes in such circumstances. We celebrated my mom's life and memory and ultimately moved on with our own lives, as each and every one of us has to in such circumstances.

There was, however, one odd thing that occurred at the time of my mom's passing. Everybody, from time to time, stumbles upon the body of a dead bird. But three times in practically as many weeks, and on opposite sides of the world? One particular morning, when I was at my dad's helping to arrange my mom's funeral, we were sitting in the living room when we heard a large thump: a blackbird had slammed into a window of my dad's house and was killed outright, crashing to the ground outside the door to my dad's conservatory. Then, the next day, when we went to my mom's nursing-home to thank all the staff for having looked after her when the Alzheimer's reached its severest of stages, there was a brightly feathered little bird dead right outside the front door to the building. And, the day after I returned to the States, I found yet another dead bird, this time on the drive, right by the front door. Maybe this whole "dead birds by the doors" saga was just the result of a series of odd coincidences and nothing else. Not everyone was quite so sure, however.

"Omens surrounding dead birds often vary according to what you find dead," said Raven Meindel, a good friend of mine and a fellow Fortean writer and researcher. "A dead dove, for instance, can mean marital strife and a need for change in the marriage. A dead songbird or other little birds of that type can mean a big change following sorrow or stress. You've certainly had your share of stress recently, my dear friend. The finds, if they are in fact signs rather than coincidence, could simply mean to take notice of the changes in life and that you may have to redirect or adjust things for a while or even permanently. The blackbird slamming into the window seems to definitely have been a messenger, as they often are the messengers of souls crossing over, so that particular one seems to have the most significance of all of them, since it was at the time of (or shortly after) your mom's passing." [1]

Whether this was all coincidence, or something more profound, I do not know. But in the two years that have now passed since my mom's death, I have not found, or stumbled upon, another dead bird.

Seeking Skinwalkers with the Stallionaires

In early August 2010, a month or so after returning from England, I was off to California in search of skinwalkers, those shapeshifting, malevolent beings from Native American lore that can take on a dizzying variety of animal forms, but that predominantly appear in the guises of wolves, owls, foxes, coyotes and ravens. According to Navajo teachings, locking eyes with a skinwalker will allow it to enter and possess both your mind and body. Evil and deadly, the skinwalker should be avoided at all costs and at all times, which meant only one thing to me: I just had to go looking for it! [2]

This wasn't an investigation I was anticipating planning or undertaking, however. Rather, it was prompted by a telephone call out of the blue from yet another TV show. This one was VH1's *Real and Chance: The Legend Hunters.* For those who may not know, Real and Chance—actually, brothers Ahmad and Kamal Givens, and two-parts of the rap group, The Stallionaires—first made their mark, not long earlier, on a VH1 dating show, *Real Chance of Love.* But it wasn't long before the quest for hot babes was traded in for a search for terrible beasts. That's right: Real and Chance were about to go monster hunting. The show ran for ten entertaining episodes and saw our heroes in hot pursuit of Bigfoot, giant hogs, marauding snakes, and—in my case—shapeshifters. I wasn't at all sure how this one was going to go down, but it turned out to be one of my all-time favorite, and most satisfying, TV-based experiences. [3]

When the production company behind the show approached me, I imagined myself deep in the heart of darkened woods, as so often seems to be the case when I'm on the trail of unknown animals for TV land. But this time the setting was the California desert, and only the very shortest of distances from the legendary Integratron and Giant Rock of famed UFO contactee George Van Tassel. A local shapeshifter was supposedly slaying and mutilating cattle and other animals in and around the nearby towns of Landers and Joshua Tree. Deep in flying saucer country, then, a predatory and savage skinwalker was on the loose. [4]

Over the course of three days and two nights, Real, Chance, and I hung out with a Native American woman who rescued wild and injured wolves, nursed them back to health in her sanctuary, and had a deep terror of not only encountering a skinwalker, but of even uttering the very word itself. Clearly, the views and fears of times past as they relate to skinwalkers are still quiet prevalent in certain, isolated, parts of 21st century California. We were taught to fire guns with actual silver-bullets by a grizzled old cowboy who answered only to the title of "Doc," and who made it clear to us that to encounter a skinwalker, careful preparation is absolutely essential. And that meant learning how to blast things to Kingdom Come, which we did for approximately three hours on a hot and sunny afternoon in some old desert canyon.

In addition, the three of us took part in Native American rituals to prepare us for, and protect us from, the deep hazards that lay ahead. We headed out to a now derelict ranch where even as far back as the early 1980s farm animals were found torn apart and partially eaten by some unknown, powerful predator. And we spent a dark night chasing *something* that stole a dead chicken—with a tracking device attached—from under our very noses and right around where the slaughtering had taken place three decades earlier.

So, did we come face to face with a skinwalker? Well, I can't say for sure. But, what I *can* say is that we really *did* find ourselves confronted by a huge, dark wolf late on the last night of the expedition. It was a majestic beast expertly captured for on-screen posterity by VH1's camera crew. For four or five minutes, the black-colored animal loomed malevolently above us on a rocky outcrop that sat atop a winding, deep and very dark cave, staring intently at us and possibly even sizing us up, it seemed. Suddenly, however, it turned on its tail and raced away into the desert darkness. That wasn't quite the end of things, however.

As we continued to scour the area, and checked out the entrance to the mysterious cave, Real, Chance, and I finally located the tracking device, minus the chicken, just inside its entrance. Since skinwalkers are said to be able to take on the specific form of wolves, and often lurk within dark caves and caverns, this might make some conclude that we actually *did* encounter a skinwalker. So, today, I'm willing to say *maybe* I confronted my nemesis that night that I spent roaming around the desert with the Stallionaires. The deep strangeness in remote Californian realms was far from over, however.

The Curious Tale of the Camel Corps
About two weeks after I got home from my adventures with Real and Chance, I received an email from an old man named Fred Goodson, who had a fascinating tale to tell that was *also* focused upon sightings of strange animals seen in and around Joshua Tree and Landers. Fred's beasties weren't shape-shifting monsters, however. Rather, they were camels! And some of them at least were ghostly in appearance. In the course of a lengthy chat with him on the telephone the next day, I came to learn that "since the turn of the '70s," Fred had been carefully researching and cataloging tales and sightings of camels in the deserts of California, Arizona, New Mexico, and parts of the Texas Panhandle. Many might scoff at the idea that there could be whole herds of camel roaming the wilder, desolate parts of the United States, but the reality of the situation is that such a scenario is actually not completely implausible. And before I get to Fred's story, I'll tell you why we can't rule out such a possibility. But to do so we have to go back in time to the mid 1800s when the U.S. Army, which was acutely aware that the weather in the deserts of the southwest could be particularly torturous at times and that its horses often did not fare well when faced with the overwhelming heat, came up with the idea of using animals that were better able to withstand the heat than horses. So why not create a U.S. Camel Corps that could be used as pack animals for the transport of sundry military items over vast arid distances? Well, that's precisely what the U.S.

Army chose to do.

As far back as 1836, during the Seminole Wars in Florida, one Major George H. Crosman chose to use camels instead of horses while fighting the Native Americans of the area, chiefly because the humped animals required very little in the way of sustenance. Problematic, however, was the fact that the Army's horses seemed to have an unfathomable fear of the camels, and as a consequence interspecies fighting became a regular, chaotic sight. Thus the camels and the horses had to be kept well apart at all times, which did pose a bit of an issue for the military.

But certain influential people in the Army took careful note that a great deal of money and resources could be saved by using camels in campaigns where the temperature was high and the ground was dry. It was during the American-Mexican war of 1846 to 1848 that this hit home with the U.S. military, when the harsh conditions really took their toll on their horses. But, there were still concerns about the feasibility of having whole swathes of the military go from using horses to largely untried and untested camels. That all changed in March 1855, however, when Congress passed a bill allowing for $30,000—a fairly impressive sum of money at the time—to be allocated to a project that would determine if the idea of a camel corps was worth pursuing, long-term, short-term, or not at all.

It scarcely needs to be said that camels are not indigenous to the United States, so this meant an overseas trip was in order for those assigned to the project. As a result, and three months after Congress approved the plan, a team working to the orders of a Major Henry C. Wayne boarded the USS Supply for a trip to distinctly exotic destinations. The entire trek took months, but finally led to Wayne's team securing 30 camels from a seller in Smyrna, an ancient city on the Aegean Coast of Anatolia, which today comprises most of the Republic of Turkey. Ten months after it left the United States, the unit was finally home, its quarry completely intact. Its first port of call was Indianola, Texas, where the first batch of camels took their first steps on American soil.

All went well initially, and the camels were used routinely by the U.S. Army throughout the Southwest on missions that would probably have ended in death and disaster had the military been wholly reliant on horses and mules, as had previously been the case.

But things changed for the worse when the American Civil War broke out in 1861. With the entire nation plunged into chaos, the military was thrown into a state of carnage, with Americans fighting and killing fellow Americans, and there was no-one around to take care of the camels. The result was that some of the camels, which by the start of the Civil War had been housed on military land in California, Texas, Arizona, and New Mexico, were sold to zoos, circuses, traveling menageries, and ranchers. A sizeable number had the good sense and instinct to make their escape, and others were secretly released into the wild by the animal-loving soldiers whose job it had been to care for them. As a result, they began to live in the wild in the deserts and woods of the southwest, along with their ever-expanding number of offspring. Sightings of the huge beasts and their descendents were reported across the Southwest for decades, with the last encounter surfacing from Douglas, Texas, in 1941. Actually, the 1941 event was the last *believed* and *accepted* date upon which such a sighting was made. But maybe it wasn't actually the last encounter, after all. And here's where we say "Hello" again to Fred Goodson. [5]

Night of the Living Dead Dromedaries
Although the final sighting of a wild camel in the United States, officially at least, occurred in the same year that the Japanese military attacked Pearl Harbor, this wasn't quite the whole story, as Fred Goodson told me. Given that I have a somewhat conspiratorial mind, I figured his tale would involve some long U.S. Army-connected cover-up to explain why there had been such a dismissal of the post-1941 accounts. But that wasn't the case at all.

The reality, Fred told me, was that while the accounts he had on record of surviving pockets of camels roaming the United States up until at least the late-1970s were certainly provocative and amazing, they simply did not pop up on the radar of the mainstream media or of the zoological community. Or even if, on a very rare occasion, someone in the press did take note of the stories, they were largely lumped with sightings of Bigfoot and ridiculed, said Fred. And today's military could hardly be blamed for not caring either, he added. After all, what was the Army to do? Spend countless tax-dollars travelling the deserts of America for years trying to track down a few herd of camel that were living quite contentedly anyway? It was simply not going to happen. In fact, no one seemed to care, except for Fred, and he cared deeply, too. That much was clear from the quivering emotion present in his voice, as he spoke on the telephone.

But there was more to come. In speaking with Fred, I could not deny that the story he had been faithfully following from his old trailer near Landers was certainly fascinating from a folkloric, historic, military, and zoological perspective. But it had little to do with my own, far more esoteric, areas of interest—until Fred told me a bit more about some of the cases that had attracted his attention. As Fred explained it, he had a network of contacts in the southwest— including military historians, veterinarians, zoologists, archaeologists, and prospectors—who from time to time provided him with snippets of data and leads on sightings of camels seen in, chiefly, California and Arizona from the late 1800s to the late 1970s, with the very occasional story surfacing from New Mexico and Texas. Then, time and finances permitting, Fred would head off into the wilderness in search of the legendary animals.

In the course of his quests, Fred came across a number of reports that, while clearly of the camel variety, weren't exactly what he was expecting. I asked Fred what he meant by that, and he told me that over the years he had received a handful of stories of camels seen in desert locales that seemed far more ghostly than they did flesh and blood. Witnesses had told Fred of camels that were semi-transparent, that vanished in the blink of an eye, that left no tracks even on soft sandy surfaces, or that, like true specters from the outer edge, faithfully haunted the same old, well-worn pathways on a regular basis.

Each and every report Fred received up until the late 1970s were of regular-looking camels. But the post-1970s reports were all spectral. There were not many such cases, just eight between 1980 and 2007. But this change in reports had led Fred to conclude that the camels had now finally, and completely, died out—physically, anyway. But perhaps they weren't completely gone. Did their spirits continue to linger amid their old desert homes?

Then there came a true bombshell. Although Fred's small body of data on the spectral camels extended from 1980 to 2007, there was, he said, a brand new spate of such activity in the vicinity of

George Van Tassel's Integratron and the nearby Giant Rock. Fred then asked me if I would be willing to come out to the desert, hang out in his old trailer for a few days, listen to his tales, and then stake out the area in case the supernatural animals returned? Of course, I would, and I did! Soon, thereafter, I was bound for California, my expenses paid for by Fred himself.

An Obsession is Born
Things began in appropriately weird and synchronistic fashion. Of all the places where Fred could have arranged for us to meet, he chose a little out of the way diner in the desert, which just happened to be the one where I was initially filmed meeting Real and Chance for the *Legend Hunters* show only weeks earlier. So, having made a 7:40 a.m. landing at California's Ontario Airport and secured a rental car, I hit the road to the café. A few hours later, I pulled up on the dusty, windswept parking area outside the café and walked in.

"You're back," said an unsmiling waitress whose face I recognized, and who obviously remembered me from the VH1 shoot, but evidently not favorably, for some unfathomable reason.

"Yep," I replied, adding: "Do you know Fred Goodson? I'm supposed to be meeting him here at noon."

"You mean the camel man?"

"Yeah, at noon."

"Yeah, he comes in at noon."

"That's when I'm meeting him."

"Well, that's when he comes."

It was a stunning conversation, absolutely stunning. I sat down, ordered a coke, and waited on Fred. And, right on the stroke of midday, in he strolled. Fred looked exactly as I had anticipated. He had a friendly, tanned leathery face, the sort of visage that develops from years spent living in harsh desert climes and working outdoors under a relentless sun. Dressed in a crisp white shirt, blue jeans, Stetson hat, and brown leather boots, he looked every inch the typical, affable old cowboy that everyone in town knows—and that's precisely what he was.

After exchanging quick greetings with about half a dozen old buddies, Fred came over, shook and crushed my hand, saying hello in enthusiastic fashion. He then ordered burgers and fries for us both, and launched into his story.

Fred explained that although he was originally from Phoenix, Arizona, he had lived a pretty much nomadic life, traveling all across the Southwest, seldom putting down long-term roots, and working variously on the railroads, as a rancher, as a crop duster, and even as a gold prospector for four years in the latter part of the 1950s. It transpired that Fred's interest in the Camel Corps Caper, as I call it, was provoked in the early 1950s by the tale of an old truck driver who had told Fred of seeing seven camels blissfully wandering across a stretch of California desert about 15 miles outside of Joshua Tree back in the early 1930s. Upon hearing the story, Fred was hooked on camels. His obsession, for it was surely that, had now begun.

After lunch, I followed Fred in the rental car to his trailer, which was located on a sandy piece of ground, just outside of Landers. Filled to the brim with files on, and photos of, camels, Fred's abode was a fascinating Aladdin's Cave for the camel connoisseur. He proudly opened up his voluminous files, which contained incredibly detailed and documented reports of camel sightings dating back decades and from all across the more barren parts of the Southwest.

"Fred," I asked, after digging deep into the impressive body of material, and taking a look at a huge map on one of the walls that detailed the various encounters he had on file, "why don't you do your own book on this? This is a *great* story!"

"Oh, I don't know," he replied, with a good-natured chuckle and some red-faced embarrassment. "One day, maybe, I will." It was then time to discuss the latest wave of encounters, which just happened to take place a stone's throw from the enigmatic Integratron.

The Saucerer's Apprentice
Brought into this world in Jefferson, Ohio, in 1910, George Van Tassel made his mark in the Contactee movement that dominated the early years of UFOlogy. Van Tassel both surfaced and peaked in the 1950s, and came close to eclipsing even famed contactee George Adamski in the popularity stakes. Close encounters with longhaired aliens, huge conferences held in the California desert, and a definite gift for spreading the sage-advice of the Space Brothers, all ensured that Van Tassel would be remembered as a legend of the saucer world of the 1950s.

Van Tassel became fascinated with aviation at a young age and, after dropping out of high school, began working at Cleveland Airport, Ohio, where he secured his pilot's license. At the age of 20, he headed for California and took a job in a garage owned by his uncle, Glen. Then fate stepped in and changed everything. While working with his uncle, Van Tassel crossed paths with a man named Frank Critzer, a German immigrant who had retired to the deserts of California due to a chronic case of asthma, and who took to prospecting the mines near the town of Landers, a community in San Bernardino County. The resourceful Critzer had hollowed-out a home for himself beneath a large rock in the area known as Giant Rock, which was deemed sacred by local, Native American Indians.

Captivated by Critzer's life as a desert prospector and adventurer, Van Tassel convinced his uncle to loan Critzer $30 so that he could purchase some much-needed mining equipment. In return, Van Tassel would receive a percentage of any profits that might be generated as a result. But it was not to be. At the height of the Second World War, rumors circulated among the close-knit community of Landers that the lonesome Critzer was a full-blown Nazi spy, undoubtedly sent to the United States to undertake some nefarious task on behalf of Adolf Hitler and his cronies. As a result of these allegations, local law enforcement officers paid Critzer a visit in 1942.

What was intended as an interview quickly turned into a showdown: Critzer, sensing danger, retreated into his carved-out home beneath Giant Rock, at which point the cops responded by throwing canisters of tear-gas into his underground lair. Big mistake: one or more of the canisters had a disastrously close encounter with Critzer's dynamite stash, and the man was blown to smithereens.

In 1947, Van Tassel quit his job as an aircraft engineer with Lockheed, contacted the Bureau of Land Management (BLM), and applied for a lease that would allow him to run the now-abandoned airstrip that was adjacent to Giant Rock. The BLM approved everything, and Van Tassel soon had a new abode, Critzer's *Flintstones*-style underground house. He was soon hard at work, redeveloping the airstrip and constructing both a café (called the Come on Inn) and a dude ranch on the property.

On moving into the cave, the Van Tassels were shocked to see the walls still stained red with Critzer's blood, or so the doubtful legend goes. Adding to the legend are the recollections of his half-sister, Margaret Manyo, who says that Howard Hughes (with whom Van Tassel had worked at Lockheed) used to fly in on weekends to indulge in the tasty pies that Mrs. Van Tassel was known to cook. All was normal for several years, but that all changed late one night in 1951, when the aliens decided it was time to get chummy with Van Tassel.

By Van Tassel's own account, he was sprawled out on the desert floor ("meditating") that night, when his astral form was transferred to a gigantic UFO that was sitting in Earth-orbit, and where he met a group of aliens known as the Council of Seven Lights, who bestowed upon him the usual Space Brotherly spiel about how humankind's forever wicked ways needed to be reeled in before irreversible, planet-wide disaster took hold.

Then, in August 1953, Van Tassel claimed he finally met the aliens in the flesh; they supposedly hailed from the planet Venus. At this historic meeting, the aliens reportedly confided in Van Tassel the means by which the average human lifespan could be massively extended. Thus was born an ambitious plan for Van Tassel to build the Integratron, a white, sixteen-sided, two-storey, domed building that allegedly had the ability to recharge and rejuvenate body cells. Van Tassel worked tirelessly on its construction for years.

The principle workings of the Integratron were two-fold: the first revolved around the reported sacred geometry of domes and their apparent ability to focus the mystical energies that emanated from the planet's depths. The second principle held that each one of us has our very own "wavelength," and that the numerous wavelengths emanating from the Integratron would resonate with ours. The result of this would be a steady and constant recharging of our basic cellular structure. In this way, potential human immortality was just right around the cosmic corner.

The Integratron was finally completed in 1959. As evidence of Van Tassel's skills, it was built entirely out of wood and concrete, and without the benefit of even a single nail or screw. The only thing lacking, very unfortunately, was the precise means by which the Integratron could influence and extend human life spans. The aliens, apparently, never came clean on that particular topic. And in true irony, Van Tassel died an old man before he could bring the entire thing to fruition. No one can say that E.T. lacks a sense of humor.

So, anyway, here I was, investigating not UFOs, but uncanny camels, at the Integratron! [6]

The Ghosts of Giant Rock

It was fortuitous that the most recent report of a ghostly camel to come Fred's way had occurred in the very area he was now living. Could someone, I wondered out loud, who was local and knew of his research, be taking him for a ride? Fred admitted that he could not dismiss such a possibility, but he thought it most unlikely. He told me the story had come from a local dirt biker who had seen a group of camels just a couple of hundred feet from him as he raced around Giant Rock early one Sunday morning in May 2010—and on two subsequent occasions also, the latest being only a couple of weeks earlier. That dirt bikers do indeed use the area on a regular basis is not a matter of any debate. Take a trip out to Giant Rock on just about any day of the week, stay for a while, watch and wait, and eventually you will see them zipping around the Mars-style landscape like huge, furious cockroaches, or like the giant, radioactive ants in the 1950s science fiction movie *Them!*

As for the camels, though, Fred's informant advised him that seeing the animals was amazing enough on its own. And, not surprisingly, he brought his bike to a screeching halt when they sauntered into view from right behind Giant Rock itself. It was all the man could do to stare in shock and awe, only to be suddenly cast aside in favor of sheer terror, when the animals vanished in the blink of an eye. And, Fred impressed on me, he *did* mean in the blink of an eye. They were gone, like *really* gone.

The biker, Fred added, could scarcely believe what he had just seen and for some time remained silent on the matter. Until, after confiding in a few friends, he learned of Fred's research and the fact that Fred lived in the very same area. So the two got together to chat about the event, as well as two subsequent sightings of the very same animals, the other occasions being late at night, however, when the group of camels were seen wandering around the Integratron under an eerie, moonlit sky.

But there was even more to the strange story. The biker, a young guy named Jordan, claimed to be a psychic with the ability to see and converse with deceased animals. Despite Jordan's initial shock when the encounter occurred, if he was speaking truthfully about his paranormal skills, then the events at Giant Rock might not have been quite so random, after all. Was such a story just too good to be true? I certainly hoped that it was not. And particularly so when Fred suggested that he, Jordan, and I should scout out Giant Rock the following night, which is exactly what we did.

Most people can't visit Giant Rock after the sun has set without being affected in some sense by its massive presence. Maybe it's the craggy Moon-like terrain, the huge monolithic form that is Giant Rock, or just the uncanny and enthralling atmosphere that desert locales always seem to provoke in the human psyche. Maybe, in my case, however, it was because I was just about to sit under the stars with a psychic who was going to try and contact the spirits of a wandering herd of spectral camels.

Jordan was 20, a rocker, and someone who appeared curiously out of place in and around Landers and Giant Rock. He looked like he should have been fronting a hard-rocking Rob Zombie-style outfit in downtown L.A. on a Friday night. But he much preferred the solitude of the desert and the spectral presence of the dead. I freely admit that I have done few investigations into the controversies of the afterlife, and so I am always largely reliant on the work of those skilled in such matters when it comes to trying to understand what's afoot. So this is why, after we drove out around 9:00 p.m. and settled down under Giant Rock's far side, I pretty much sat back, listened, and carefully absorbed the evening's events.

To say that the night was a dark one is not an exaggeration. Deep in the desert, far away from any sort of the overpowering light pollution that so dominates much of our world, things look acutely different. All I can say is that it's very good we had powerful flashlights with us. Giant Rock, the surrounding sloping peaks, the floor, and the horizon—everything was *black*. I would actually say beyond black, if such a thing were possible. But eventually our eyes became accustomed to the darkness.

Jordan suggested the three of us should close our eyes, focus on the image of the legendary camels crossing the old desert, and mentally try and contact them with one goal in mind: to have them manifest in our midst. Personally, although I tried hard, I felt or experienced nothing at all, other than excitement and anticipation. Fred felt much the same. Jordan's experience was very different, however.

Twenty minutes or so into the experiment, Jordan said four chilling, words: "It's started; they're coming." Fred, somewhat worried, quickly asked what had started and, more importantly, what was coming, but Jordan motioned him to stop, and said: "Let me focus on it first." So, Fred and I sat back and watched as Jordan leaned back against the great old rock that Van Tassel called home, and seemed to enter some odd, altered state of mind full of whispered noises that sounded vaguely word-like, distinct head shaking, much hand wringing, and the occasional severe jerk that one might associate with getting hit hard by a Taser. For five or six minutes Fred and I watched the extraordinary spectacle, after which Jordan began to slowly return to normality. Both Fred and I were eager to know what had happened.

The Last of the Camels

Fred lit a fire, cracked open three beers, and the story came tumbling out in spectacular fashion. According to Jordan, in no time at all his mind had been filled with clear and undeniable imagery of the collective memories of the U.S. Army's Camel Corps. Jordan told of seeing amazing images of the Army's original overseas expedition to secure the original batch of camel back in the 1800s. He spoke vividly and with deep emotion about psychically experiencing the horrors of the Civil War, as well as uplifting scenes of military personnel whose job it was to care for the animals, choosing to release them into the wilderness lest they become nourishment for starving, underfed soldiers. And Jordan also told of the upswing in the emotional states of the animals themselves as they began to embrace and enjoy their newfound freedoms at the height of the Civil War. Then the imagery suddenly jumped to the early years of the 20th century. Jordan elaborated that he found his essence, or soul, soaring high across the deserts of the Southwest and could see herd after herd of camel, admittedly small in number, but healthy and vibrant (a) near the Rio Grande, (b) on wild land near Corona, New Mexico, and (c) only ten or so miles from our current location.

"This," stated Jordan, "was their happiest time: free and roaming, in an environment they loved." Things then suddenly became far more solemn. As the 20th century progressed, expanding towns, growing human populations, and an increasing struggle for adequate resources meant that the camel populations began to noticeably dwindle in both number and geographic distribution. Jordan added, in solemn tones, that the last of the camels took its final breath in a desolate remote part of Nevada in 1977. Regardless of what Fred might wish to believe, said Jordan, any and all tales of camels seen roaming the United States post-1977 were either bogus, examples of mistaken identity, or genuine events involving spectral animals. And that was it: story over.

We sat and pondered upon the extraordinary experience for a few hours. Could it all have been the work of Jordan's subconscious and imagination, unknowingly trying to offer Fred some reassurance that his years of work had not been in vain? Jordan, somewhat noticeably defensively, was sure that was not the case. He was positive that, in some poorly understood fashion, he had actually channeled the memories and souls of the old, long dead camels, those whose ghostly forms still forever roamed these parts. And maybe Jordan did precisely that. Whatever the truth of the matter, it clearly had a positive effect on Fred, it deeply affected Jordan, and was one of the most profoundly weird and memorable experiences I have ever played a part in, albeit as a bystander and observer, rather than as a central player. Even after our chat was over, we sat in silence for some time, chugging back our beers, wondering about those old, largely forgotten camels, and musing on one of the strangest and most surreal episodes in the history of the U.S. Army.

I left Fred, homeward bound, early the following morning. As I drove out of town for Ontario Airport, I pondered Fred's final words as we said our farewells: "I'm not going to stop. And, you know what? I *am* going to write that book!" Having by then come to know Fred's deep enthusiasm for his quarry, which easily paralleled, and maybe even eclipsed, Captain Ahab's quest for the mighty whale in Herman Melville's classic novel of 1851 *Moby Dick,* I didn't at all doubt it. After spending the best part of 40 years chasing and researching the descendents of the U.S. Army's long-gone Camel-Corps, it was about time Fred got some decent, worthwhile payback. And, just maybe, one day, I thought, Fred will be able to say with

Chapter 9
Chasing the Chupacabras

"The creatures of the night will soon be surfacing."

A Curious Canine

On a hot and sunny afternoon in September 2010, I was sitting in a barbecue joint in the little Oklahoma town of Norman, munching down on a huge turkey sandwich. Opposite me was a woman named Jaclyn Schultz, a news anchor with Fox News in the Sooner State. Sitting next to her was a cameraman named Ben. The three of us were deep in discussion about a strange beast that was then said to be roaming around the fringes of a high school in the nearby town of Tecumseh. The beast was one of the legendary Texas Chupacabras—creatures about which a great deal has been said, written, and overwhelmingly misunderstood and misinterpreted in the process. It was time to try and set the record straight about the beasts and their calamitous activities. In other words, we were about to shoot a segment for Fox News that suggested that the hairless, dog-like monsters of the Lone Star State had found a new place to call home. But before I get into all that, some background data on the creatures is most definitely required. [1]

Ever since the mid-1990s, sensational stories have surfaced from the forests and lowlands of Puerto Rico that tell of a fearsome creature roaming the landscape by night and day. The animal has been described as having a pair of glowing red eyes; powerful, claw style hands; razor sharp teeth; a body not unlike that a monkey; a row of vicious spikes running down the length of its back; and, just occasionally, a pair of large and leathery bat-like wings. And if that is not enough, the beast is said to feed on the blood of the local animal population—predominantly goats—after puncturing their jugular veins with two sharp teeth. That's correct: Puerto Rico has a monstrous vampire in its midst. Its name is the Chupacabras, a term that, very appropriately, translates as Goat Sucker.

Theories abound with respect to the precise nature of the beast, with some researchers and witnesses suggesting that the monster is some form of giant bat. Others prefer the theory that it has extraterrestrial origins. The most bizarre idea postulated, however, is that the Chupacabras is the creation of a top secret, genetic research laboratory hidden in Puerto Rico's El Yunque rainforest, which is located in the Sierra de Luquillo, approximately 40 kilometers southeast of the city of San Juan. [2]

On five occasions now, I have traveled to the island of Puerto Rico to seek out the vampire-like Chupacabras for myself. Today, the mystery remains precisely that, a mystery. However, the controversy was given an unexpected boost midway through the 2000s, when rumors began to surface that the Chupacabras had somehow made its way to the Lone Star State! [3]

Following a lecture I gave to the San Antonio chapter of the Mutual UFO Network (MUFON) in November 2008, legendary UFO researcher Walt Andrus produced from his briefcase a skull that he explained was from a Texas Chupacabras. According to Andrus, who is a native of Schertz, Texas, an associate, who had shot the completely hairless animal on nearby ranchland some months earlier, had given it to him. Several weeks later, John Schwab, who runs the San Antonio chapter of MUFON and is an Andrus colleague, mailed the very same skull to me, which, in October 2009 was filmed at my house by a team from the National Geographic Channel's *Paranatural* series. They were then in the process of making a documentary on the Chupacabras of both Texas and Puerto Rico. [4]

But before we get to my excursion to Oklahoma with Fox News, a few insightful words on the nature of the Texas Chupacabras from my good friend and fellow monster-hunter Ken Gerhard. Few have worked harder than Ken to separate fact from fiction and rumor from folklore when it comes to the Lone Star State equivalent of Puerto Rico's most famous monster.

"I first learned of the Texas Chupacabras from Jon Downes in 2004," says Ken. "As we sat and drank cold Shiner Bock beer in the courtyard of San Antonio's haunted Menger Hotel one evening, Jon told me about how he had been driven to a town called Elmendorf earlier that day, in order to meet a rancher named Devin McAnally. Apparently, Mr. McAnally had dispatched an inexplicable, bluish-gray animal that had been slaughtering his chickens. After looking at some photos of its strange corpse, Jon had deduced that the creature was obviously some type of canine, but beyond that he was unable to make a definitive identification." [5]

Ken continued: "People often ask me, are the Texas Chupacabras merely mangy coyotes? To simply say 'Yes' is an oversimplification, I personally feel. Examination of their physical remains, and DNA tests and analysis, has confirmed that these animals belong to the genus Canis. It's also true that the closest genetic matches have been with coyotes; though the Elmendorf Beast may have been a hybrid. It seems plausible to theorize that an extreme type of mange is being passed from mothers to their offspring, causing their hairless condition. My associate, naturalist Lee Hales, has pointed out that adaptations happen all of the time in nature. And maybe their baldness has even given them an advantage on the hot plains of Texas. Perhaps it is even being written into their genetic code." [6]

But there seems to be far more going on. "As of yet," Ken astutely noted, "no one has been able to sufficiently explain their other abnormal characteristics, which have included grossly enlarged fangs and claws, irregular skulls, disproportionate limbs, and unusually long tails. These are all traits that seem inexplicable. These creatures might possess cataracts in their eyes, resulting in poor vision. This would certainly explain why so many of them have been shot so easily, or run over by cars. There is also the issue of their sinister behavior, which seemingly revolves around lapping up the blood of helpless poultry. There could be specific nutrients in blood that these animals crave, due to their affliction." [7]

Despite all the years of study, as Ken admits, we are still left with one, overridingly important question: "Exactly what are these blue, zombie dogs that roam the grasslands of Texas?" This is the very question that was being pondered upon by a certain trio of adventurers not in Texas, but in Oklahoma, during the latter part of September 2010. [8]

The Terror of Tecumseh

Perhaps as an ominous precursor of what would follow, on May 10, 2010, Tecumseh was struck by a devastating tornado that damaged three churches and more than one hundred homes, some severely. And out of this storm-driven carnage and chaos, a Texas Chupacabras emerged, large and malevolently.

As the Fox team and I arrived in Tecumseh, a small town of

barely 6,000, situated in Pottawatomie County, Jaclyn told me that a Tecumseh High School student named Ryan Craighead had seen a strange beast roaming around the fields and woodland near the school in the summer of 2010. It was not a normal looking wild animal. Dog-like in its form, but utterly devoid of any body hair, it possessed a pair of extraordinarily short front limbs that, as the creature ran, reminded Ryan of the hopping motion that one would expect to see in a kangaroo, rather than the conventional gait of a coyote. After seeing the animal on a number of occasions, Ryan finally managed to capture it—on his cell phone camera. Jaclyn opened up her cell phone and showed me the priceless picture. Incredibly, while the animal did resemble the so-called Elmendorf Beast; the ridiculously short front limbs it possessed made it clear that this was not just a coyote with a bad case of mange. It was almost as if the animal had been grossly mutated at a genetic level. I have to say, I was pretty impressed.

The three of us then made our way to a field near the school where, with the sun now bearing down upon us, I covered myself in sunscreen and practically masked my head and face with a bandana and sunglasses. Jaclyn began by asking me about my views on the Chupacabras, my various excursions to Puerto Rico, and my thoughts on what the Texas—and now the Oklahoma—Chupacabras might really be. When we got to the topic of whether or not we stood even a degree of chance of resolving the mystery, given that we were there for one afternoon and night only, I said that we would do our very best. Little did I know it at the time, but our very best actually turned out to be pretty good!

By around 6:15 p.m. we had secured all of the background footage, and it was now time to scout out the area. Our first stop was Tecumseh City Lake. As I told Jaclyn, any wild animal in the area would require three key things to survive: cover, food, and water. The lake and its immediate surroundings undoubtedly provided all three in abundance. As we reached the water's edge, we could see numerous prints that, to the untrained eye, might have been interpreted as those of a Texas Chupacabras. What they were actually were pretty large alligator tracks! We got some good footage, kept a careful watch on the deep water in case the beast that made the tracks decided it was time for a bit of dinner of the human variety, and then went on our way.

By 7:00 p.m., the sun was beginning to set. "The creatures of the night will soon be surfacing," I said in my best atmospheric tones for the benefit of Ben's camera. As we began to search the area, Jaclyn phoned Ryan Craighead, who had taken the priceless picture that had led me on my trip to Tecumseh, and he agreed to come along and show us exactly where the action had taken place. Twenty minutes later, he and a friend were on the scene. As we set up the cameras, Ryan told us how he had spotted the beast on several occasions, and how utterly amazed he was by the weird, short, front limbs that it possessed, as well as the way it seemed to hop around the fields, all the while keeping a careful distance from the students and the hustle and bustle of the school.

Thirty minutes later, nightfall was almost fully upon us. But before it got really dark, we hit pay-dirt. In a dried-up stream that bordered a small but dense area of woodland, we found numerous paw prints that were coyote-like in appearance. This strongly suggested that while our quarry may have been grossly mutated in a fashion that was very far from clear, somewhere within its monstrous form there existed a fairly significant amount of coyote DNA. The fact that the tracks were clearly recent was a very strong indication the beast was still prowling around. I suspected, too, that it was strongly aware we were on its tail, metaphorically-speaking, and maybe even literally, too.

Fifteen minutes or so later, we were in overwhelming darkness. Fortunately, Ben had night-vision equipment, and so we were able to continue on our quest for the terror of Tecumseh. And I think we came very close to doing just that. As Jaclyn and I knelt down and chatted in whispered tones for the camera, a coyote-style howl reverberated all around the area. That sent the local dog population into a frenzy of crazed barking. Spurred on, we continued to scour the whole area, again finding tracks and hearing the ominous cry that is the typical calling card of the coyote.

There was no denying that the beast was now among us, but it remained one step ahead of us at all times, before eventually disappearing into the darkness, never to return—or, at least, not on that night. We waited a while, but when the wild cries were finally no more, it became clear that the animal had tired of our games and had headed ever deeper into the woods or fields. Jaclyn and Ben were very pleased with the evidence we had secured, however, and we shared our thoughts on the quest, then said our collective goodnights and headed back to our respective homes. I got back to Arlington around 2:15 a.m. with thoughts of the hairless monster swirling around my head. A month or so later, the footage captured on that memorable night aired on Fox News in what turned out to be a good, solid feature. It was a job well done. [9]

Chapter 10
Owlmen Everywhere

Rocking at the Rock – Again

December 2010 was a month that I will long remember. It represented a particularly memorable period when my pursuits of strange beasts reached a peak of high strangeness. First, I spent a week in the early part of that month once again out at Giant Rock with a bunch of fellow pursuers of everything odd and otherworldly, including Greg Bishop, author of *Project Beta*; Andy Colvin, who has penned an ever-growing series of books on Mothman; Robert Larsen, radio-host and, with Greg Bishop, one of the founders of *The Excluded Middle* magazine; Chica Bruce, author of such books as *The Philadelphia Experiment Murder* and *Celestial Secrets*; Walter Bosley, former U.S. Air Force Office of Special Investigations operative and writer; and Adam Gorightly, author of *The Prankster and the Conspiracy* among other books. We were a satisfyingly odd and multifaceted bunch.

The purpose of the excursion was to make a television documentary with an Australian crew about some of the more Fortean aspects of southern California. Inevitably, a trip to Giant Rock was the order of the day, or rather, it was the order of several days. We made Landers and Joshua Tree our bases of operation for pretty much the entire period. It was a memorable time: I got to spend a night alone in the very motel room in Joshua Tree where early 1970s music legend—and good friend to the *Rolling Stones'* guitarist Keith Richards—Gram Parsons died. There was an old store in town that had six-foot-tall metallic sculptures of long-necked dinosaurs and a Tyrannosaurus Rex on display. And while out in the desert, we stumbled upon a bit of enigmatic graffiti that read: "Give Humanity A Chance. Sasquatch." I was not sure if this was a message meant *for* Bigfoot, or if we were intended to actually believe that Bigfoot had written it *for* us! Either way, the synchronicity of half a dozen or more Forteans finding such a monster-themed message out in the desert was certainly not lost on us during the course of those surreal few days of filming out at Giant Rock. But there was something more, too.

I was intrigued to find at Giant Rock a large spray-painted face on one of the nearby rocks of what looked just like the visage of the infamous Owlman made famous in Jon Downes' in-depth study of the beast, *The Owlman and Others*. When I called over Andy Colvin—our expert on what appears to be the U.S. equivalent of the Owlman, namely Mothman—to take a close look at this piece of crypto-owlish graffiti, he commented almost immediately that this was a sign of, well, something significant, and that we should now expect to see a resurgence of not just interest in the legendary Owlman, but possibly even new sightings of the beast itself. Though I listened carefully to what Andy had to say, and took note of it, I promptly, and unfortunately, forgot all about it. That is, until just a few days later, when a whole range of Owlman and owl-related madness exploded across the internet and my email inbox.

Clelland's Comments
Mike Clelland is the keeper of *The Hidden Experience* blog, much of which is focused upon Mike's personal paranormal experiences, synchronistic events, and odd encounters in his life. About ten days after I stumbled upon the Owlman artwork at Giant Rock, Mike wrote at his blog: "Last week I saw an owl on a telephone post. I was walking to my car on a cold winter night, after leaving a friend's house. At the time I was in a somber emotional mood. It felt like I was in confusing point in my life. I stood directly under the owl for a minute or so, and it watched me from above but never flew off. The next afternoon my friend (who's house I left the previous night) saw a Great Gray Owl on a post right outside her window. Earlier that day, she had received an emotional email from an old boyfriend, and when they were dating they both had lots of curious owl sightings, including owl dreams! I'm not sure what any of this means, but I feel obligated to pay attention." And, as Mike also noted, he felt compelled to write this the very night before he was due to conduct an interview with none other than Mothman expert, Andy Colvin! [1]

Naomi and the Owlman

On December 23, my good friend Naomi West, who with her husband, Richie, undertakes a wealth of work in the U.S. for Jon Downes' Center for Fortean Zoology, related the following: "As with every Christmas season, I have been receiving books I've requested. As with every day of the year, I'm already behind on books I have been intending to read. I'm currently undertaking everything Orson Scott Card (OSC) has ever written, but because I'm kind of a slow reader due to some degree of attention deficit that will likely take me a couple years.

"Two weeks ago, I was concentrating my energies on *Ender in Exile*. Richie had just bought OSC's latest (*Pathfinder*), so that was next on my list, followed by Anne Rice's latest angel book. That would take up the next three months for sure, and that's not including my plans to continue reading *The Ender* series with my uncle.

"Suddenly, for no reason I can identify, I dropped everything and began reading *The Owlman and Others* by my friend Jonathan Downes. Why in the world I chose now, halting my already ambitious reading plans, to pick up this book that had been in my possession for two years is mysterious to me, but why I would choose the Christmas season to immerse myself in the part of cryptozoology that deals with the more sinister side of the unknown is even stranger." [2]

But there was even more to come in the saga of all things owlish and the life of Naomi.

A New Witness Surfaces

Naomi's email continues: "Richie and I are presently at my mom's for the Christmas holidays. Two days ago (and two weeks into my Owlman book) we received a phone call from MUFON (Mutual UFO Network) for whom we are field investigators. This was an unusual case they were assigning us to: an apparent man-bird sighting in San Antonio. MUFON does not typically address cryptid sightings, but a lady who, with her husband and son, had seen a giant man-bird flying over her neighborhood back in April had just decided to report it to MUFON.

"I find it nothing short of bizarre that the report this of sighting—the first of its type that has ever come my way—would occur the very time I had chosen, for no known reason, to read a book on this very thing. I cannot believe this is coincidence. As George Noory [the host of Coast to Coast AM] says, there is no such thing."

As for the report that Naomi and her husband Richie received and which they forwarded on to me, it reads as follows: "I was talking on my cell at the end of my sidewalk by the street when I turned around facing my house and saw this huge black man bird thing gliding without a noise...

"When I saw this I was stunned and stared at it trying to figure out what it was and then I saw it wasn't anything I've ever seen. I ran into the house and yelled at my husband and my grown son to get out here quick. They came but seemed like forever and they looked and saw it too. When they saw it the thing was like the a few streets over and then disappeared behind the big trees. When we saw it we all said that no one would believe us; but I have recently been talking about it because it has bothered me so much.

"I lived in this neighborhood all my life and I can remember of three UFO sightings since I was five and all the sightings were in this neighborhood or around Stinson Field airport. I never came forward about them because people think ya lost your ever loving mind until recently when others I've spoke with shared their experiences.

"I have other stories but this one is the most recent and I was wondering if anyone has ever seen this thing. It is silent like it was a glider but I could see the body was exactly like a man a very large man. Thank you for listening to me and I hope you don't think we have gone mad too. I called my daughter and told her afterwards and that's what made my mind up to stay silent. I had my darn cell on my the whole time and not once thought of taking a picture it happened so fast and I'm not that savvy on the cell." [3]

The sighting took place in San Antonio, which just happens to be the home of Ken Gerhard, author of *Big Bird!* His book deals with sightings of anomalous, winged monsters and flying men in the United States and elsewhere, including Owlman-like entities. The foreword to Ken's book was written by Owlman authority, Jon Downes, who also happened to be the editor and publisher of *Big Bird!* And still the weirdness was not over.

The Monster Reaches London
Four days after Naomi's story surfaced, Oregon-based anomalies

researcher and writer Regan Lee noted that Penhaligon's, a perfume store in London, England, had created a new advertising campaign centered on something called the Olfactory Owl. Basically, the beast was a man, dressed in old-style Victorian clothing, who sported the head of an owl, and roamed the streets, subway-stations and trains, and shopping malls of London, advertising Penhaligon's perfumes. A man with the head of an owl: Owlman! [4]

Barely 24 hours later, a London-based researcher named Davy Allen contacted me with a report of a strange, flying man seen over London's River Thames six days earlier. This would have placed the occurrence right around the time Naomi West and Mike Clelland were focusing on Owlman and owls. In this case, while the details were unfortunately very scant, the witness told Allen that he had seen a "massive, big man with wings like a bird, hovering over the river and shot into the sky and vanished." Like the Owlman and Mothman, the London beast, said Allen, had a pair of bright, glowing, red eyes. [5]

On December 27, 2011, exactly one year to the day after Regan Lee's story of the Olfactory Owl surfaced, Naomi West wrote me in response to my inquiry about using her Owlman-linked accounts in this book. After confirming that she had no problem with me using the story, Naomi added: "It's funny you mention this now because I was JUST reminded of that Owlman-synchronicity story this week when I got [Andy Colvin's] *Mothman Speaks* [book] for Christmas. As always, I'm reading several different books and I had the sudden urge to just drop everything and read it instead. I didn't, but I was reminded of that." [6]

I told Naomi of the one-year anniversary issue regarding Regan Lee's post, to which she replied by email: "Ha! The synchronicities seem to be never ending." Andy Colvin was spot-on with his words at Giant Rock. The Owlman, it seems, is destined and determined to stay with us. [7]

Chapter 11
The Taigheirm Terror

"Finally, appeared a cat of a monstrous size,
with dreadful menaces."

The Cat Files

In early February 1998, the British Government's House of Commons held a fascinating and rather unique debate on the existence or otherwise of a particular breed of mystery animal that is widely rumored to inhabit much of the British Isles, the so-called Alien Big Cats, or ABCs, as they have become infamously known. It scarcely needs mentioning that Britain is not home to an indigenous species of large cat of the puma variety. Nevertheless, for decades amazing stories have circulated from all across the nation of sightings of large, predatory cats that savagely feed on both livestock and wild animals and that terrify, intrigue, and amaze the local populace in the process.

The controversy in the House of Commons began with a statement from Mr. Keith Simpson, at the time the Member of Parliament for mid Norfolk: "Over the past twenty years, there has been a steady increase in the number of sightings of big cats in many parts of the United Kingdom. These are often described as pumas, leopards or panthers. A survey carried out in 1996 claimed sightings of big cats in 34 English counties."

In response, Elliot Morley, who was the then Parliamentary Secretary to the Ministry of Agriculture, Fisheries and Food, added: "It is impossible to say categorically that no big cats are living wild in Britain, so it is only right and proper that the Ministry should continue to investigate serious claims of their existence—but only when there is a threat to livestock and when there is clear evidence that can be validated. I am afraid that, until we obtain stronger evidence, the reports of big cats are still in the category of mythical creatures." [1]

Thanks to the Freedom of Information Act, we now have that stronger evidence. Replying in 2006 to a FOIA request from a member of the public with an interest in big cat sightings seen in the county of Hampshire between 1995 and 2005, the county's police force released previously secret files that stated: "Hampshire's Constabulary's Air Support Unit has been deployed to assist with the following reports: January 1995 – Black Panther like animal seen in Eastleigh. Two likely heat sources found by the aircraft, but nothing found by ground troops. March 1995 – Black Puma like animal seen in Winchester. One heat source found that could not be classified by the aircraft crew, kept running off from searching officers, search eventually abandoned." [2]

Notably, when a similar FOIA request was filed with Sussex police in late 2005, documentation was made available to the requester that read as follows: "Firearms officers have been deployed in response to such a report on one occasion, on 22 July 2004 – sighting by a member of the public in Seaford. The area was searched, but no trace was found of such an animal." [3]

The story is far more spectacular on the east coast of England, however. In 1991, official documents show, a lynx was shot dead near Great Witchingham, Norfolk, by a man who then placed the body in his freezer before selling it to a local collector who decided to have the creature stuffed and mounted. The Department for Environment, Food and Rural Affairs believed that the lynx may have escaped from a zoo, although this was never actually proven. It transpires that an extensive, secret dossier on the affair was opened by local police that would have remained under lock and key were it not for the useful and illuminating provisions of the Government's Freedom of Information Act.

The story began when police officers were investigating a gamekeeper who, it was strongly suspected, may have been responsible for the deaths of a number of birds of prey that had been living within the area. The officer that interviewed the man in question wrote in his now declassified official report: "At the start of the search in an outhouse, which contained a large chest freezer, I asked him what he had in the freezer, and he replied: 'Oh, only some pigeons and a lynx.' On opening the freezer there was a large lynx lying stretched out in the freezer on top of a load of pigeons! He had shot this when he saw it chasing his gun dog." [4]

Britain's exotic cats, it seems, are no longer the myth that many people want them to be or believe them to be—and the government knows it full well, too. But is there even more to the puzzle? And could the mystery get even stranger?

Britain's Supernatural Felids

I am personally convinced that the overwhelming majority of Britain's big cats are flesh and blood animals that have successfully managed to survive and thrive in the countryside for decades or more. Researcher Neil Arnold has suggested it may have been going on for centuries. There are, however, more than a few incidents that, for some people who have been personally exposed to the controversy, seem to suggest far stranger points of origin for at least *some* of the cats in question. Quite a few such rogue reports emanate from an area of central England that I have often written about: the Cannock Chase woods, a veritable hotbed for activity of the werewolf, Bigfoot, ghostly black dog, and big cat variety.

Eileen Allen says that she caught sight of a "big black panther," as she described it, while walking in the woods in the latter part of 1996. But the overwhelming shock of seeing the immense beast staring intently in Allen's direction was nothing compared to the absolute terror that struck her when the creature quite suddenly and literally vanished into thin air while making a sound that Allen described as "like an electricity cracking noise." Unsurprisingly, Allen did not hang around, and quickly left the woods. To this very day, she has never returned, nor does she have any plans to do so anytime in the future. [5]

Bob Parker experienced something very similar in the woods in 2000, barely a quarter of a mile or so from where Eileen Allen had her encounter four years earlier. In Parker's case, the sighting occurred while he was walking his dog on a Sunday morning. As he did so, a large black cat came hurtling violently through the heather, skidded onto the pathway that Parker was following, and bounded off, apparently not at all bothered or concerned by the presence of either Parker or his little Corgi dog named Paddy. Seeing a big cat was astounding enough in itself, but what happened next was downright bizarre and unreal.

"Me and the dog just froze solid," said Parker. "I couldn't believe it, could *not* believe it. But when [the cat] got about fifty feet from us, it sort of dived at the ground. It sort of took a leap up and almost dive-bombed the path, and went right through and vanished, just like that. I know exactly how it sounds, so you don't need to tell me, because I had a belly-full from the missus about it all for ages. But that's exactly what happened. It was like it just melted into the path." [6]

Equally strange, but for very different reasons, is the story of Sally Ward. While walking with her husband across the Cannock Chase not too far from Milford Common on a wintry and very foggy morning in the 1960s, she claims that they stumbled upon what she described as "a black panther, a real one" that was sitting "bolt-upright" on an open stretch of ground to their left, and approximately 30 feet from them. But that was not the strangest spectacle. Also standing upright around the huge beast was what Ward described as "seven or eight other cats. But normal cats, pet cats."

She was absolutely sure that the smaller animals were not "big cat kittens," but were "the sort of cats anyone would own. I don't know anything about panthers and lions and tigers, but I know a normal cat when I see one, thank you very much." Rather strangely, all of the smaller cats were staring, in almost hypnotic fashion and in complete silence, at the large black cat, as if utterly transfixed by its proud stance and powerful, muscular presence.

The Wards, perhaps quite naturally, felt very ill at ease with the situation, and both slowly and cautiously continued past the group, and then raced down to their car, which they had parked in Milford. Ward's husband wanted to report the encounter to the local constabulary, but after Mrs. Ward pleaded otherwise, they decided to remain silent, aside from quietly confiding in various friends over the years. To this day, Sally Ward stands by her story with total conviction: "No one will ever tell me there isn't something funny about the black panthers in England." [7]

Distinctly maverick cases such as these are, for many big cat researchers in Britain, the absolute bane of their subject, simply because they suggest that at least some of the nation's mystery cats may be much more, or paradoxically far less, than flesh and blood animals. And for that reason, investigating them can be highly problematic. It is one thing to say that big cats are prowling around the wilds of the British Isles. But it is quite another thing altogether to suggest that some of the creatures may very well have paranormal or supernatural qualities.

So how do we even begin to explain and reconcile such reports? *Can* we even explain and reconcile these accounts at all? Well, maybe. But to do so, we have to first go back in time to 1976 and the ancient English counties of Devon and Cornwall. And then, having done that, we will take a wild ride even further back into history, specifically to Scotland's Isle of Mull and a series of infernal rites and rituals that may possibly go some way towards explaining the small number of truly strange and anomalous big cat encounters in Britain—and maybe even those elsewhere, too.

The Dark Words of Downes

As practically each and every British soul aged about 40 and upwards will graphically recall, midway through 1976 the good folk of the nation were pummeled into exhaustion and submission by what was one of the hottest summers on record for many a decade. I was only 11 at the time, but I still have vivid memories of how, in August of that year, water supplies came perilously close to completely drying-up; of people who were seemingly dropping like flies from the effects of heatstroke; and of the rumors flying around that the British Army would take control of the streets if the fabric of society should begin to unravel and crumble. That the Sex Pistols' anthem, "Anarchy in the UK," would be released just a few months' later, only served to add to the apocalyptic atmosphere enveloping the nation. Fortunately, such a nation-collapsing scenario did not come to pass, and the extraordinary weather eventually gave way to what generally passes for normal in the British Isles: rain, wind, and dark grey skies. And everyone, I am sure, breathed a distinct sigh of relief when the sun finally elected to move on to pastures new. I know I certainly did. That same year was famous, or rather infamous, for a whole variety of things beyond just the bizarre weather, however.

It was also in 1976 that one of the most monstrous of all cryptozoological creatures emerged wildly out of the woods that surround Mawnan Old Church in Cornwall, England: the ominous Owlman. The terror-inducing, glowing-eyed, and feather-winged entity that could very easily pass for the Mothman's transatlantic cousin became the absolute talk of Cornwall for months, and ultimately sent the Center for Fortean Zoology's director, Jon Downes, on a dark quest that came perilously close to destroying him, both mentally and physically. And if that was not nearly enough, from the depths of the waters off the coast of Cornwall surfaced a veritable serpent of the deep: Morgawr, a southwest equivalent of the Loch Ness Monster, if ever there was one. But there was far more high strangeness afoot in this time-frame and locale, and absolutely none of it was of a positive nature at all.

And no one was able to better chronicle this strange affair than my old mate and partner in cryptozoological crime, Jon Downes himself: "Cats were disappearing from Redruth, Falmouth, and Penryn over the summer. According to a representative from the Cat's Protection League, abnormally large numbers of cats were missing from their homes. The spokesman for the charity claimed that they were being sold to vivisectionists; but that is a common story used to explain such spates of missing creatures, and is I feel, unlikely to be true." [8]

Jon continued: "Cats are among the easiest creatures in the world to breed. There is never any shortage of kittens free to a good home, and were vivisectionists, or cat-furriers, to want a supply of such animals, it would be extremely easy to arrange a constant supply without the need of breaking the law. It is also unlikely that the market forces would demand a particularly large number of such animals; and it is almost certain that any hospital, research laboratory, or chemical firm worth its salt would buy their experimental animals from reputable suppliers rather than from the sort of shady character who would attempt to make a living from selling stolen pears." [9]

Jon also noted: "Spates of missing cats almost certainly have a different explanation, but they are of great interest to the Fortean. It is a well known fact that the number of missing cats rises according to the number of sightings of alien big cats [known as ABCs] in the vicinity. Zoologists who believe in such things will claim that this is because pumas—the animals most likely to be responsible for the vast majority of 'genuine' (whatever that means) ABC sightings—are partial to the taste of their smaller, domesticated cousins." [10]

Demons of the Taigheirm

There is another explanation for the sightings of giant, mystery black cats and their associations with everyday pet cats. It is an explanation that takes some very strange twists and turns and has at its black heart a vile and disturbing conspiracy that extends across the centuries, throughout the higher echelons of power, and that is truly evil in nature. An ancient rite borne out of darkest and ancient Scotland, it is called the Taigheirm. It's something that had a profound impact on me in December 2010.

Merrily Harpur, a British big cat researcher and the author of *Mystery Big Cats*, said of the Taigheirm: "This was an infernal magical sacrifice of cats in rites dedicated to the subterranean gods of pagan times, from whom particular gifts and benefits were solicited. They were called in the Highlands and the Western Isles of Scotland, the Black-Cat Spirits." [11]

The rites in question, Harpur added, "involved roasting cats to death on a spit, continuously for four days and nights, during which period the operator was forbidden to sleep or take nourishment, and after a time infernal spirits would appear in the shape of large, black cats." [12]

Without doubt the most detailed description of this archaic and highly disturbing rite can be found in the pages of J.Y.W. Lloyd's 1881 book, *The History of the Prince, the Lord's Marcher, and the Ancient Nobility of Powys Fadog and the Ancient Lords of Arwystli, Cedewen, and Meirionydd*. Since Lloyd's words are vital to understanding and appreciating the weird story that will soon unfold in its unsettling entirety, I make no apology for quoting the author at length: "Horst, in his *Deuteroscopy*, tells us that the Highlanders of Scotland were in the habit of sacrificing black cats at the incantation ceremony of the Taigheirm, and these were dedicated to the subterranean gods; or, later to the demons of Christianity. The midnight hour, between Friday and Saturday, was the authentic time for these horrible practices and invocations; and the sacrifice was continued four whole days and nights, without the operator taking any nourishment." [13]

On this matter, Horst himself said of the cruel rite: "After the cats were dedicated to all the devils, and put into a magico-sympathetic condition, by the shameful things done to them, and the agony occasioned to them, one of them was at once put alive upon the spit, and amid terrific howlings, roasted before a slow fire. The moment that the howls of one tortured cat ceased in death, another was put upon the spit, for a minute of interval must not take place if they would control hell; and this continued for the four entire days and nights. If the exorcist could hold it out still longer, and even till his physical powers were absolutely exhausted, he must do so.

"After a certain continuance of the sacrifice, infernal spirits appeared in the shape of black cats. There came continually more and more of these cats; and their howlings, mingled with those roasting on the spit, were terrific. Finally, appeared a cat of a monstrous size, with dreadful menaces. When the Taigheirm was complete, the sacrificer [sic] demanded of the spirits the reward of his offering, which consisted of various things; as riches, children, food, and clothing. The gift of second sight, which they had not had before, was, however, the usual recompense; and they retained it to the day of their death." [14]

Lloyd took up the story from there: "One of the last Taigheirm, according to Horst, was held in the island of Mull. The inhabitants still show the place where Allan Maclean, at that time the incantor, and sacrificial priest, stood with his assistant, Lachlain Maclean, both men of a determined and unbending character, of a powerful build of body, and both unmarried. We may here mention that the offering of cats is remarkable, for it was also practiced by the ancient Egyptians. Not only in Scotland, but throughout all Europe, cats were sacrificed to the subterranean gods, as a peculiarly effective means of coming into communication with the powers of darkness.

"Allan Maclean continued his sacrifice to the fourth day, when he was exhausted both in body and mind, and sunk in a swoon; but, from this day he received the second-sight to the time of his death, as also did his assistant. In the people, the belief was unshaken, that the second-sight was the natural consequence of celebrating the Taigheirm." [15]

At this point in his narrative, Lloyd elected to quote Horst: "The infernal spirits appeared; some in the early progress of the sacrifices, in the shape of black cats. The first glared at the sacrificers and cried 'Lachlain Oer' [Injurer of Cats]. Allan, the chief operator, warned Lachlain, whatever he might see or hear, not to waiver, but to keep the spit incessantly turning. At length, the cat of monstrous size appeared; and, after it had set up a horrible howl, said to Lachlain Oer, that if he did not cease before their largest brother came, he would never see the face of God. Lachlain answered, that he would not cease till he had finished his work, if all the devils in hell came. At the end of the fourth day, there sat on the end of the beam, in the roof of the barn, a black cat with fire-flaming eyes, and there was heard a terrific howl, quite across the straits of Mull, into Morven." [16]

Lloyd himself then continued: "Allan was wholly exhausted on the fourth day, from the horrible apparitions, and could only utter the word 'Prosperity.' But Lachlain, though the younger, was stronger of spirit, and perfectly self-possessed. He demanded posterity and wealth, and each of them received that which he has asked for. When Allan lay on his death-bed, and his Christian friends pressed round him, and bade him beware of the stratagems of the devil, he replied with great courage, that if Lachlain Oer, who was already dead, and he, had been able a little longer to have carried their weapons, they would have driven Satan himself from his throne, and, at all events, would have caught the best birds in his kingdom.

"When the funeral of Allen reached the churchyard, the persons endowed with second-sight saw at some distance Lachlain Oer, standing fully armed at the head of a host of black cats, and every one could perceive the smell of brimstone which streamed from those cats. Allan's effigy, in complete armour, is carved on his tomb, and his name is yet linked with the memory of the Taigheirm.

"Shortly before that time also, Cameron of Lochiel performed a Taigheirm, and received from the infernal spirits a small silver shoe, which was to be put on the left foot of each new-born son of his family, and from which he would receive courage and fortitude in the presence of his enemies; a custom which continued till 1746, when his house was consumed by fire. This shoe fitted all the boys of his family but one, who fled before the enemy at Sheriff Muir, he having inherited a larger foot from his mother, who was of another clan. The word Taigheirm means an armoury, as well as the cry of cats, according as it is pronounced." [17]

In 1922, Carl Van Vechten commented on this particularly nightmarish ritual in a footnote contained in his book *The Tiger in the House*. It reads: "The night of the day I first learned of the Taigheirm I dined with some friends who were also entertaining Seumas, Chief of Clann Fhearghuis of Stra-chur. He informed me that to the best of his knowledge the Taigheirm is still celebrated in the Highlands of Scotland." [18]

Keeping this point firmly in mind, consider the following thought-provoking question from Merrily Harpur: "Could the 'Black Cat Spirits' which the Taigheirm produced be linked to the presence of huge black cats seen on Mull in the present day?" [19]

Certainly, for such a relatively small and remote place that is entirely separated from the Scottish mainland, Mull has experienced a number of memorable sightings of big black cats over the course of the last few decades. Investigative researcher and writer Glen Vaudrey learned that one such sighting was made in 1978 by a Mrs. G.W. Brodie and a friend. Vaudrey related the details of the Brodie encounter: "When she described the sighting in 1985, she would state that at first glance they thought the animal was a black dog; perhaps a Labrador. But then it crossed the road, and started to climb over some rocks heading up to the foothills of Ben More. As it moved, it became apparent that the animal was not a dog after all, but a large black cat."

Two decades later, adds Vaudrey, "a couple [was] driving around the north side of Loch na Keal where they had been filming otters. As they drove along, they became aware of a large cat sitting upon a ridge above the road. They first noticed it as it looked down in their direction. They stopped the car and attempted to stalk the cat, but to no avail— it was having none of it, and quickly moved off into the trees."

The same couple had a *second* sighting only a couple of months later. This time the location was the south side of Loch na Keal, and it took place as the beast was attempting to stalk a group of sheep, although in a rather lackluster fashion. Vaudrey stated: "Two reports from the area seem pretty extraordinary, but how about a third? This one was made by a group of three people holidaying on Mull in October 2003. The three of them were driving through Gruline heading back from the Ross of Mull at around 3:00 p.m. For those who are not familiar with the geography of the Isle of Mull, Ggruline is to be found at the head of Loch na Keal. Do you see a pattern forming here?"

As to the beast itself, Vaudrey explained: "What they reported seeing was an animal that they described as looking like a large cat, which was either very dark or black in colour, that was stalking along the grass verge at the side of the road…The consensus of opinion was that it appeared to be a puma…" And with respect to the Taigheirm and the big cats of Mull, Vaudrey commented: "Perhaps it is an echo of that act that has created the mystery big cat of Mull." [20]

So much for Mull, but what if there is more than mere echo of it at work elsewhere? What if a modern day incarnation of the Taigheirm still exists? Could that explain some manifestations of modern day mystery big cats in Britain and elsewhere?

Chapter 12
Slaughter in Dallas

"I wish I had better news."

The Cat Conjurers on the Move

In early December 2010, right after my latest excursion to Giant Rock, I was briefly back to my place of birth: ye olde England. While there, I met up with a man named Don Johnson (not of *Miami Vice* fame), who had contacted me a few months earlier and claimed that the disciples of the Taigheirm were still up to their old tricks today, not on Scotland's Isle of Mull but in Staffordshire, England, however. Johnson said he knew parts of the fantastic saga, and that his words would make me finally realize the true, paranormal nature of many of Britain's big cats. So what else could I do but listen to what the man had to say?

The meeting with Johnson occurred in a pleasant old tavern in the Staffordshire town of Rugeley, on the fringes of the Cannock Chase woods, prime big cat territory. Basically, his story went like this: for many years, Johnson's now deceased father worked for an esteemed, powerful, and wealthy Staffordshire family, and over time he had worked himself up to a position of some standing within its ranks. It was around 1982, however, that something undeniably disturbing occurred.

Johnson's father was invited to attend a Saturday night cocktail party held at a large old mansion that was reportedly situated just outside of the town of Stoke on Trent. It's here that he was presented with a near-Faustian offer. Several close colleagues of Johnson's father's were also in attendance, and their manner suggested they were fully aware of the nature of the cold offer that was about to be placed upon the old, oak table. When the sun had set and the group of about 12 retired to a sprawling lounge, the reason for the invite became horrifically clear.

Rather casually, Johnson's father was asked: "Have you ever heard of the Taigheirm?" He replied that, no, he had not, which is not at all surprising. After all, how many people have? As a result, there followed (a) a lengthy and detailed history of the Taigheirm; (b) an explanation of how the cat sacrifices were still being undertaken at secure, well-guarded locations in Staffordshire; and (c) dark revelations concerning their purpose, and how, allegedly, if the sacrifices were conducted strictly according to the ways of the old and now largely forgotten gods of ancient Britain, the resultant effect could be considerable wealth, as well as power and influence, for the successful conjurer. This was all very reminiscent of the tales about the Beast of the Bodalog Farm I heard in the Crown pub in Rhayader in the summer of 2009.

To his credit—or not, depending upon your personal perspective—Johnson's father was utterly appalled at the very idea of it all and immediately said that he wanted no part of what sounded very much like "devil worshipping in one of them old Hammer films." And for those who have seen it, Hammer Films' *The Devil Rides Out* most definitely springs to mind.

In response, the group merely thanked Johnson Sr. for listening to their offer, assured him ("only half-jokingly," according to a deadly-serious Don Johnson) that he need not worry about "anything happening to him, like a car accident," and relative normality was restored via a few more drinks and discussions of a lighter, more down to earth nature. Johnson's father worked closely for another four years with several of the people who were in attendance at the party, but the disturbing matter of the Taigheirm was never again brought up—very much to his relief, said Don Johnson. And it was not until the early 1990s that Johnson was guardedly told the story by his then terminally ill father, who finally decided to reveal the truth.

But, as I had suspected would be the case, Johnson had come to one, perhaps inevitable, conclusion: namely, that at least *some* of the curiously elusive big black cats said to be roaming Staffordshire were not flesh and blood entities at all. Rather, Johnson suspected that their beastly presence was due to the effects of Taigheirm-like ceremonies that were still being secretly conducted by powerful men and women all across Staffordshire under the safety blanket of the night, all for reasons directly relevant to personal, financial, and sexual gain.

Cat Capers in the Woods

Don Johnson claimed intimate knowledge of several people allegedly engaged in the present day rites and sacrifices in Staffordshire—one of whom, he said, was a well known figure in "the county's politics" in the late 1980s—but he declined to identify any of them by name, somewhat conveniently, the skeptically-minded might well say. Nevertheless, Johnson did, admittedly, have a couple more interesting things to say. First, he directed me to a story that had appeared in Staffordshire's *Chase Post* newspaper in 2000, and that focused on a big cat sighting on the monster-infested Cannock Chase. [1]

The story told of a then 68-year-old man from the Chase-surrounded town of Hednesford who steadfastly declined to be named by the *Chase Post*, but who had seen a large cat in the area on two occasions. He carefully recalled that "One Monday lunchtime a few weeks ago I was driving home from Ingestre Park Golf Club when this cat jumped over the hedge then pounced over the ditch. This cat was about 18 to 20 inches high with a long, thick black tail." When the man then informed the staff at the golf club of the incident the following day, they responded in underwhelming fashion. "I assured the woman I had not been drinking," the man said, "but she didn't seem bothered." [2]

Two or three weeks later, the man saw the animal, or a very similar one, again as he was heading for the gold club. The time was roughly 6:30 p.m., and it was already getting dark when his headlights picked up something at a distance of about 50 yards: "I saw a pair of green eyes in the hedge. I tooted my horn at it and it ran off." Somewhat oddly, he added: "Since then I have heard a lot of people are walking with big torches around there. Last Monday I saw about ten people who appeared to be searching for something." [3]

Precisely who these flashlight-wielding, mysterious characters were remained a puzzle to both the witness and the staff of the *Chase Post*. For Don Johnson, however, they were nothing less than a secret offshoot of the ancient Taigheirm, undertaking unspeakable rites designed to provoke the presence of monstrous, grotesque cats as part of some devilish bargain that would bring untold treasures and delights to those involved in the invocations. But it was what Johnson had to say next that practically floored me.

"You live in Dallas, don't you?" Johnson asked.

"Well, yeah, nearby; you know that. I'm in Arlington," I replied.

He pondered for a moment, but then dropped a bombshell: "Did you know there is an American equivalent of the Taigheirm—government people mainly—and they have a Dallas group that operates out of White Rock Lake?"

I was stunned into silence for a moment. Was this a joke? Dallas' White Rock Lake was the place where I had made my home from January 2004 to June 2008. I have mentioned this fact in previous books, so it's possible that's why Johnson brought up White Rock Lake. As the story progressed, however, I found such a scenario less and less likely.

Constructed in 1911 as Dallas's first reservoir, White Rock Lake has nine and a half miles of shoreline, thick trees, and a path for walkers and cyclists. It is home to an estimated 33 types of mammal, including squirrels, rabbits, skunks, raccoons, possums, bobcats, red foxes, and minks, and 54 varieties of reptiles, including rattlesnakes, turtles, a variety of lizards, and horned toads. Salamanders and frogs also abound, along with an incredible 217 bird species, including swans, pelicans, sea gulls, loons, and all manner of ducks.

Admittedly, the lake *was* a mysterious place. Surrounding it are tales of UFOs, a ghostly hitchhiker, car-sized catfish, huge alligators, and Goat Men similar to the one seen at Lake Worth, Texas, in the summer of 1969. But the Taigheirm? *Really?* I challenged Johnson to offer up some form of proof of his outrageous claim. He merely suggested, somewhat enigmatically, that I take a closer look at what was going on at White Rock Lake, including the mysterious deaths of countless pet cats in the surrounding vicinities. I assured Johnson I would do precisely that. I anticipated finding nothing at all. How utterly wrong I was. [4]

The Taigheirm Hit Texas

When I returned to the States a few days later, I spent a week or so chatting with various friends and colleagues in the world of Dallas-based journalism, some on local newspapers and others on community-themed magazines. Without bringing up the controversy of the Taigheirm, I asked if any of them had heard stories of unusual cat killings in the area. I've always found—whether it's in Britain, the United States, Canada, Puerto Rico, and pretty much everywhere else I've lived and worked—that hooking up with local media sources and plying them with a few potent brews is not only good for developing work-oriented leads and increasing one's income, but it also helps a person to forge friendships and stay informed of breaking and developing stories. This is precisely what happened when I began looking into the saga of the cat mutilations of Dallas, Texas. I was totally amazed to find that such reports were widespread and had even attracted the attention of the Dallas Police Force, which viewed the matter with deep concern.

In the summer of 2008, for example, two cats had been found dead—dissected in truly grisly fashion—in the area of Dallas' Lovers Lane. Rather curiously, so-called "lovers' lanes" all across the world are absolutely notorious for attracting paranormal phenomena and supernatural legends. Then, in July 2009, the local *Advocate* magazine reported on the horrific killing of a cat in Dallas' Lakewood Heights. The person who had the misfortune to stumble across the carnage on his front lawn, a man named Geoffrey Ley, told *Advocate* staff: "The cat was literally cut in half at its midsection. There was no blood on our front lawn; so it appears that the mutilation probably occurred elsewhere and the remains were dumped on our lawn by the perpetrator." As a result of the publicity, the Dallas SPCA put up a $5,000 reward for any information leading to a conviction. No one was caught, however, and the reward money was never collected. And matters only became worse as time went on. [5]

In the days and weeks that followed the violent attack at Lakewood Heights, still more cats were found dead, butchered systematically with great precision, this time in Dallas' Midway Hollow, which prompted police to take a more proactive role in the controversy. Senior Corporal Kimberly Crawford said: "We used to think it was a juvenile up to no good. But now we think it might be an older guy who lives nearby, snatches these cats, mutilates them, then takes them back to where he finds them. I wish I had better news." [6] Then, in August, Ken Kalthoff, of NBC-DFW, reported that at least six cats had been recently found killed and mutilated, all in Northwest Dallas. [7]

By all accounts, or as far as can be ascertained, 2010 was mercifully and thankfully quiet, but in April 2011, things began to heat up yet again. Both the *Dallas Morning News* and DFW

Animal Rescue were quick to get in on the act. *Dallas Morning News* journalist Nancy Visser reported on the discovery of a mutilated cat in the Wilshire Heights region of Dallas. As with the 2009 event at Lakewood Heights, the cat had been carefully severed at its mid-section. Notably, Visser recorded that Dallas Animal Services had been regularly monitoring animal cruelty cases and had noticed a trend over the past few years that, as each spring arrived, more and more cats were being found mutilated in the Northeast region Dallas. Despite the continuing lure of a $5,000 reward, the perpetrators remained unfound. [8]

Certainly the most bizarre aspect of this story came from a person who, commenting online, asserted that the cat mutilations were the work of the all-powerful Skull & Bones group, founded at Yale University, New Haven, Connecticut, in 1832. The commenter added it was no coincidence at all that former President George W. Bush, who was a Skull & Bones member just like his father, had made his home in *very* nearby Preston Hollow, Dallas, when his second presidential term came to a close. When I read this, I could not help but to think back to Don Johnson's assertions that the members of the Taigheirm were very powerful people in equally very powerful places—*including government.* Keeping the Bush connection and proximity in mind, I actually found myself wondering if those powerful places included the secret, inner sanctums of the White House. [9]

But if the Taigheirm data supplied by Don Johnson was correct, and if regular pet cats were being mutilated in and around the Dallas area as part of some ancient Taigheirm-type ritual, then shouldn't we also have seen some evidence of their more paranormal, and much larger, feline equivalents surfacing, too, as a direct result of the rites being undertaken? Yes, we should have. *And, just maybe, we did.*

During the early hours of a Sunday morning in July 2010, Dallas was thrown into a state of total frenzy when reports surfaced from the vicinity of the city's Union Station that two security guards, as well as several passengers on the DART train, had seen a pair of fully grown tigers roaming the area! Both the Dallas Zoo and the Fort Worth Zoo were contacted, as was the owner of a circus that was in town, but none of them reported any of their animals being missing. Police were quick to play down the sensational story, too, and suggested all of the eyewitnesses had probably been mistaken by nothing more than the presence of a couple of fairly sizeable and well-fed bobcats. Nevertheless, this didn't stop officers from diligently patrolling the nearby streets with guns drawn, dispatching to the skies of the still largely sleeping city a chopper armed with a powerful searchlight, and warning local homeless people to watch out. [10]

Was this incident really just a case of mistaken identity? Or were the exotic cats seen prowling around Dallas in the dead of night really Taigheirm-created nightmares, born out of the terrible slaughter and sacrifice of innocent pet cats in the months and years leading up to it? Maybe only the perpetrators and the curiously well-informed Don Johnson knew the answer to that unsettling question. Those responsible for the cat killings were, unsurprisingly, saying nothing whatsoever, and Johnson preferred to say no more and maintained a respectful, if enigmatic, silence. So, I decided to take the bull by the horns and see what I could find out for myself.

For three days and nights, I drove back and forth from my Arlington home to Dallas, a journey of only about 25 miles each way, and checked out some of the prime locations of cat carnage, including Lakewood Heights, Midway Hollow, Wilshire Heights, and Lovers Lane. Roaming around the streets dressed totally in black, armed with a digital-recorder and a camera, and knocking on doors with numerous questions about slaughtered cats and occult-based groups, caused me nothing but untold amounts of hassle— chiefly from worried locals who wanted to know what I was doing asking such questions. I told them, quite honestly, that as a journalist and author I was checking out the stories with a view to writing something revealing about these events. The majority of people living in the areas clammed up and preferred not to comment at all, which did not surprise me in the slightest. Most profitable, however, were the contacts I made in local coffee shops, bars, gas stations, and restaurants, many of whom remembered the attacks and mutilations very well.

The picture I was able to put together was an unsettling one, filled with brief periods of fear, paranoia, police roaming the streets after dark and hoping to catch the perpetrators, worries about whether or not "a child might be the next victim," and rumors of "devil worshippers" secretly moving into the neighborhoods. But strangest and most interesting of all was the story of a restaurant owner near Lovers Lane, who whispered two things to me that really got my attention. At one point, Dallas police had someone in their sights for the Midway Hollow attacks, but that they had been mysteriously ordered to "back off" by powerful city figures who said they would "take care of it" – wording the man flatly refused to elaborate upon. Secondly, it seems the staff at several of the local food outlets in the area had been quietly asked by the police if they had any suspicions about their "meat suppliers" possibly being implicated in the cat mutilations.

So with that information in hand, I contacted the Dallas police and asked them for an on-the- record comment. I got one, of sorts, anyway. It was a conspiratorial mixture of "no comment," "case closed," and, for all intents and purposes, "go away." It seemed to me that officialdom's role in the investigation of the affair, as well as the issue of being persuaded to look the other way by shadowy, influential figures, ran far deeper than many had previously recognized.

As for Don Johnson, well, he says that the truth of the matter is destined to surface no later than the end of 2013. It is at some point during that year, Johnson estimates, he will have completed a full-length book on the matter, tentatively titled *Supernatural Sacrifice*, that will finally reveal the truth about the big cats of Britain and their perceived paranormal origins, and provide a mass of additional data on an incredible network of active Taigheirm disciples in locations all across the British Isles, the United States, France, Russia, Canada, Australia, Sweden, Norway, Chile, and China. Or so Johnson earnestly maintains. [11]

Chapter 13
Monsters and the Government

"It was the figure of a man with wings like a bat"

It Came From the Pentagon!

There must be very few people in the cryptozoology and UFO communities who have never heard of the so-called Flatwoods Monster, or Braxton County Monster, of 1952. The story was told in-depth in Frank Feschino's 2004 book, *The Braxton County Monster: The Cover-Up of the Flatwoods Monster Revealed*, where he stated: "On the night of September 12, 1952, a shocked American public sought answers when strange unidentified objects were seen flying through the sky over Washington, DC, and the eastern United States…One of the strange objects crash-landed on a rural hilltop in Flatwoods, West Virginia." Feschino also noted that a group of schoolboys were witness to the descent of the device and, with two adults, "headed off to look for the object." [1]

According to the witnesses, however, more than a UFO was seen. A monster, estimated to be around 12 feet tall, put in an appearance. UFO investigator Kevin Randle said: "What they saw was not an animal, but some sort of creature, at least in their perception…They could see no arms or legs, but did see a head that was shaped like an ace of spades. That was a description that would reoccur with all these witnesses. No one was sure if there were eyes on the creature, or if there was a clear space on the head, resembling a window, and that the eyes were somehow behind the that window and behind the face." [2]

Not surprisingly, the group fled, terrified to the core. And although a posse returned to seek out the beast from the dark skies, it had vanished. Nearly 60 years later, the legend remains. So what was the monstrous entity: a cryptid, an alien, or a paranormal beast of some kind? Just maybe, it was something else entirely.

In September 2010, there appeared to me to be a new development in the Flatwoods Monster story. That's when I obtained a newly released copy of an April 14, 1950 RAND publication titled

The Exploitation of Superstitions for Purposes of Psychological Warfare, written by Jean M. Hungerford for the U.S. Air Force. In reading the file, I was fascinated by the accounts of how officials had successfully manipulated a wide range of paranormal mysteries and supernatural experiences for specific military advantage during the early-to-middle twentieth century. Such tactics even included the spreading of fabricated sightings of the Virgin Mary, chiefly to try and convince the hierarchy of the Soviet Union that the United States had God on its side. [3]

But, what really caught my eye, as I carefully studied the pages of the document, was a section that quoted from a book titled *Magic: Top Secret*, which was written in 1949 by one Jasper Maskelyne, a fascinating character who was up his neck in new and novel ways to fool the enemy during the hostilities with the Nazis of 1939-1945. Hungerford quoted Maskelyne about a truly alternative psychological warfare operation that occurred during the Second World War, one that eerily paralleled the strange events at Flatwoods nearly a decade later: "Our men were able to use illusions of an amusing nature in the Italian mountains, especially when operating in small groups as advance patrols scouting out the way for our general moves forward. In one area, in particular, they used a device which was little more than a gigantic scarecrow, about twelve feet high, and able to stagger forward under its own power and emit frightful flashes and bangs. This thing scared several Italian Sicilian villages appearing in the dawn thumping its deafening way down their streets with great electric blue sparks jumping from it; and the inhabitants, who were mostly illiterate peasants, simply took to their heels for the next village, swearing that the Devil was marching ahead of the invading English." [4]

The impact of this event was considerable: "Like all tales spread among uneducated folk (and helped, no doubt, by our agents), this story assumed almost unimaginable proportions. Villages on the route of our advance began to refuse sullenly to help the retreating Germans, and to take sabotage against them; and then, instead of waiting for our troops to arrive with food and congratulations of their help, the poor people fled, thus congesting the roads along which German motorized transport was struggling to retire. The German tankmen sometimes cut through the refugees and this inflamed feeling still more, and what began almost as a joke was soon a sharp weapon in our hands which punished the Germans severely, if indirectly, for several critical weeks." [5]

I was flabbergasted by the parallels between this story and Flatwoods. First, the height of the Flatwoods Monster and the British Army's devilish scarecrow were the same: 12 feet. Second, the captivating cover of Frank Feschino's book shows the Flatwoods Monster emitting lights. And the 12-foot-tall scarecrow in Italy gave off "frightful flashes and bangs" and had "great electric blue sparks jumping from it," rather like the beast of Flatwoods. Third, the RAND report specifically referred to this Italian escapade as being prepared for psychological warfare planners in the U.S. Air Force. And, in his book on the beast of Flatwoods, Feschino noted that the Air Force took careful and secret interest in the Flatwoods affair and what was being reported by the media. Fourth, the RAND report was submitted to the Air Force in April 1950, and Flatwoods occurred in September 1952. And, finally, there was also the issue of the settings: the British Army's operation was focused on little, isolated villages in Italy. And Flatwoods is a small, rural town in Braxton County, West Virginia, that even today has a population in the hundreds.

Is it possible, I wondered, while puzzling and pondering over all this, that in this two-year period USAF psychological warfare planners created their very own version of the British Army's giant, flashing monster to try and gauge what its reaction might be when unleashed upon an unsuspecting populace in the United States? But why would the U.S. Government or military wish to do such a thing?

It just so happens that a friend of mine, Rich Reynolds, an astute commentator on the UFO controversy, has a theory about all this. "The evidence is overwhelming," he says, "that there's a real UFO presence. And, back in the late forties, and at least to the sixties, I think the government knew something, or had some evidence for, the possibility of a real alien confrontation that might happen. But before it did happen, they were trying to see, and needed to see, what the public's reaction would be: would there be a panic? Would the Russians be able to take advantage of something like that? Before the confrontation happened, the CIA—or whoever—contrived these things. In the context of a military experiment, it might have allowed them to study the public's possible reaction to created events and real events" [6]

If Rich is correct, the people who suspect that the Flatwoods Monster was some form of cryptozoological creature or alien being might very well be in for a big wake-up call!

The Batman of Houston
Also in September 2010, I received a new report of a creature whose exploits were briefly legendary in and around Houston, Texas, only one year after the Flatwoods affair occurred. Certainly one of the most bizarre of all the many and varied strange beings that are said to haunt Texas is what's known as the Houston Batman. The quintessential encounter, as reported within the pages of the *Houston Chronicle* newspaper at the time, took place during the early morning hours of June 18, 1953.

Given the fact that it was a hot night, 23-year-old housewife Hilda Walker, and her neighbors, 14-year-old Judy Meyer and 33-year-old tool-plant inspector Howard Phillips were sitting on the porch of Hilda's home, located on East Third Street. "Suddenly," Walker recalled, "about 25 feet away, I saw a huge shadow across the lawn. I thought at first it was the magnified reflection of a big moth caught in the nearby street light. Then the shadow seemed to bounce upward into a pecan tree. We all looked up. That's when we saw it."

Walker went on to describe the entity to the newspaper reporter: "It was the figure of a man with wings like a bat. He was dressed in gray or black tight-fitting clothes. He stood there for about 30 seconds swaying on the branch of the old pecan tree. It had the exact appearance of a man dressed in a tight fitting uniform similar to a paratrooper. He was encased in a halo of light." The trio all agreed that the being stood about six and a half feet tall and was engulfed by a yellowish glow. The "Batman" vanished when the light slowly faded out, and right about the time Judy screamed out.

"Immediately afterwards," said Walker, "we heard a loud swoosh over the house-tops across the street. It was like the white flash of a torpedo-shaped object... I've heard so much about flying saucer stories and I thought all those people telling the stories were crazy, but now I don't know what to believe. I may be nuts, but I saw it, whatever it was... I sat there stupefied. I was amazed."

Meyer told the newspaper that, "I saw it and nobody can say I didn't."

Philips stated: "I can hardly believe it. But I saw it. We looked across the street and saw a flash of light rise from another tree and take off like a jet."

Walker reported the incident to local police the following morning. [7]

As a long-time resident of Houston, Ken Gerhard made attempts to locate the address on East Third Street where the event took place and discovered that it is no longer in existence, seemingly having been overtaken by the expansion of nearby Interstate 10. A number of years after he first heard about the exploits of the Batman, however, a close friend of his told him about some fellow employees at Houston's Bellaire Theater, who claimed to have seen a large, helmeted man, crouched down and attempting to hide on the roof of a downtown building one night during the 1990s. [8]

This story resembles one I heard about on September 14, 2010. It was one of a "flying man" seen over Houston only days earlier. Just like the Batman seen back in the 1950s, the 2010 event involved a brightly lit entity "wearing a military uniform." And, as with the 1990s-era case related to Ken Gerhard, the 2010 Batman "was wearing some kind of a helmet," but it was one that "flashed," in much the same way of the Flatwoods Monster of 1952 and Jasper Maskelyine's World War II "scarecrow" flashed. [9]

I can't help but wonder if the 1950s skies over Houston had been—and still are today—the staging grounds for yet more military-originated psychological warfare operations involving strange flying, flashing entities.

The Rogue Rats of Roswell

In early November 2010, I gave a lecture at the Emily Fowler Library in Denton, Texas, on the subject of a book I co-wrote with Ken Gerhard earlier that year called *Monsters of Texas*. The lecture was organized by Lance Oliver of the Denton Area Paranormal Society (DAPS), with whom, in early 2008, I went on a Bigfoot and Goat-Man hunt, as described in my book *There's Something in the Woods*. As is usually the case when I do lectures, I allow time afterwards for a question and answer session, and audience interaction. As a result, I was told a couple of interesting stories about large, exotic cats seen around Texas, a tale of a giant catfish, and several accounts of out-of-place or oversized animals in the Lone Star State. But the strangest of all stories flummoxed even me. That it came from Oliver himself, and was linked to the infamous Roswell, New Mexico, UFO crash of July 1947 only made things stranger.

As everyone with knowledge of the controversial Roswell affair will be aware, when the odd event occurred, certain materials found at the site of the crash were flown to Carswell Air Force Base, Texas, which is bounded on the north by Lake Worth. In 1969, this lake became briefly infamous for its sightings of the legendary Goat-Man. The story told by Oliver at the Emily Fowler Library was second or third-generation hand, so, yes, we are delving into friend-of-a-friend territory. With that in mind, the story was that when the mysterious debris was flown to Carswell from Roswell, so was "something else" that had been found in the large field of wreckage.

That "something else," Lance had been told by a source with inside information on the matter, was a pack of large, rat-like animals, which appeared to be very intelligent, moved and acted in group fashion, and were highly vicious. And that was about it: a fragmentary story of strange proportions that linked UFOs with strange animals. Whether or not the tale had even the merest grain of truth to it, or if was just some odd, folkloric rumor, neither Oliver nor I have any idea. But that's the story, for what it's worth.

It's interesting to note, of course, that theories for what really happened at Roswell aren't just focused on tales of UFOs that titillate the flying saucer research community, or secret "Mogul" balloons of the type that the Air Force stubbornly insists came down at Roswell. My very own *Body Snatchers in the Desert* book, for example, suggest that the affair had far more to do with secret, high-altitude balloon experimentation involving human guinea-pigs undertaken in the New Mexico desert. And there's another thing: we know, too, that the military was testing all manner of vehicles (including captured German V-2 rockets) at the New Mexico-based, ultra-secret White Sands facility. Some of those early flights had payloads that included monkeys, mice, and other animals. [10]

I couldn't help but speculate, as I drove home from the Emily Fowler Library, if at least a part of the Roswell legend was born out of the secret launch and crash of such a craft carrying a payload of rats aboard? Given what we know about the early experiments to place mice at high-altitudes and near-Earth orbit, maybe this tale of strange, rat-like animals taken to Carswell Air Force Base in the summer of 1947 was based upon distorted memories of real, very terrestrial rats taken to the base after the crash of a secret military device with such critters aboard. I couldn't rule out such a possibility. And I still don't.

And there's one final thing on this matter: in 2009, I secured, via the Freedom of Information Act, a series of newly declassified files from the FBI. Those files told the story of how a young boy died in the late 1940s from the effects of a rat-bite in Lincoln County, New Mexico, which just happens to be the very county where the Roswell debris was found. Not only that, but there were fears on the part of the FBI that the boy had died of "plague," and that the plague may have resulted from the actions of Japan's notorious Unit 731, whose activities also feature heavily in *Body Snatchers in the Desert*. Even more intriguing, the official FBI files on the young boy's death from a rat-bite right where the Roswell crash occurred were shared with Air Force Intelligence, the Atomic Energy Commission, and even the director of the CIA! Was something truly strange afoot near Roswell that involved Unit 731, plague-infected rats, and the launch of some secret device that remains the subject of a government-orchestrated cover-up decades later?

Roswell, I could only conclude, as I made my way back home, remained just about as enigmatic as ever. Rats! [11]

Chapter 14
Ripping Yarns

"It was 'the work of an hypnotized ape.'"

Flogging a Dead Horse

Something that seems to typify the life of a road-tripping Fortean is that even if you're not looking for it or expecting it, information, data, and new leads on old, intriguing cases just keep on surfacing. Such was the case in February 2011, when I was thrust into a strange affair that occurred more than a century ago, but that just never seems to go away despite many and varied attempts to lay it to rest. But, before I get to the meat of the tale, I first have to take you back in time to my early teens.

For many years, I have had a deep interest in the phenomenon of animal mutilations. It is an interest that began back in 1977, a year that, as far as I am concerned, was dominated by three things: the Sex Pistols' savage and overwhelmingly justified attack on the British monarchy, namely, their punk-rock classic "God Save the Queen" that was released in May; the farcical Silver Jubilee of Queen Elizabeth II in June; and my first year as a teenager, in November. I can still vividly recall playing the Sex Pistols' classic tune endlessly on my old turntable, while my dad looked on with great approval, and my mom valiantly tried to smile sweetly, wondering what on earth had happened to her little boy, who had transformed into a spiky-haired, 13-year-old lout, wearing a white t-shirt adorned with one word written in black: Destroy. But my formative years were not quite behind me, as I will now explain.

I spent my earliest years living in a pleasant, and very old, little village situated in the green pastures of central England called Pelsall. And when I say that Pelsall is old, I actually mean it's *ancient*. Pelsall was first mentioned in a charter of 994 AD, when it was among various lands donated to a monastery in the nearby town of Heantune—which today is called Wolverhampton—by one Wulfrun, a legendary Mercian noblewoman. At this time, the village was called Peolshalh, meaning "the land between two streams belonging to Peol." Later on, the *Domesday Book* described Pelsall as being wasteland, still belonging to the Church, and having been devastated in 1069 by King William's forces when they were dealing with an uprising that followed the Norman conquest of the country. Very little is known about life in Pelsall over the course of the next few centuries, aside from the fact that a chapel was built there around 1310, and that by 1563 it boasted of a mere 14 homes. You may wonder where I am going with this brief and somewhat obscure history lesson. Bear with me, as all is about to be revealed.

Pelsall eventually began to grow, and its earliest claim to real fame came in 1794, when an extensive system of canals was built on the desolate open moorland that dominates much of northern Pelsall to this very day, and which is now known as the North Common. As a result of the creation of the canals, and the discovery of a rich and valuable seam of coal shortly thereafter below those moorlands, industry soon began booming. In addition to the mining activity, a large ironworks was also established on the North Common, and which thrived for decades. [1]

By 1977, however, both the old mines and the ironworks were firmly exhausted and long gone. But for me and my mates, a bunch of kids who used to spend the six-week-long summer holidays riding our bikes around the neighborhood and trying our absolute very best to have Hardy Boys-style adventures, the ancient moorland and the ruined remnants of times past were irresistible lures. Nearly every day, we would get up early, rendezvous in the center of Pelsall, grab a few drinks and snacks, and then furiously cycle up to that magical locale, one that could quite easily have doubled for the wilds of Dartmoor, as most famously portrayed in Sir Arthur Conan Doyle's classic Sherlock Holmes novel, *The Hound of the Baskervilles*. [2]

We spent hours racing along the old canal towpaths, speeding along the ancient trackways, checking out the ruined cottages, and digging up the literally hundreds of old Victorian-era glass bottles that peppered the area and which were among the few remaining pieces of evidence demonstrating that the North Common was once a hive of bustling industry. But on one morning in August 1977, as I raced around the moors with my comrades-in-arms—Dave, Dave, Timothy and Jeremy—we came across a shocking sight: a large, muscular horse lying on its side, dead as a doornail, and with a deep

MONSTER DIARY

cut on its ribcage. At 12 years of age, I don't think any of us had ever seen a deceased animal of such a huge size before, and we simply sat on our bikes, staring at it for a minute or so, open-mouthed, shocked, and probably even quite a bit excited.

Shortly thereafter, we hit the road and quickly told numerous other friends of our find. Inevitably, word got around Pelsall about the "dead horse up on the moors." Very soon, or so it seemed, all the local kids were on the scene, eagerly ogling the rapidly rotting carcass of the immense beast, holding their noses to fight off the noxious smell of quickly advancing decay, and wondering how it had died and from where it came. None of us really knew for sure. But, one person *did* claim to have the answers.

If I ever learned the name of our informant, it has been lost to the fog of time. But what I can say is that he was an elderly, wizened, white-haired man who we often saw wandering the old canal paths and grassland, always with a large walking-stick in his hand and a faithful sheepdog at his side. Obviously, his attention had been captured by the sight of 20 kids all standing in a circle, all eagerly staring at the dead horse. And, as a direct result, he came over to see what the fuss was about.

I distinctly recall that everyone was kind of wary of the old walker of the moors and thought of him as a sinister wizard or druid-type, no doubt one who was up to his wrinkled neck in late-night occult action. At least, that's what we assumed, and we most definitely liked to assume. Yes, we were an odd and rum bunch. In reality, and in retrospect, however, he was likely just someone who had retired from work and enjoyed taking his dog for a daily stroll. But that lure of adventure on our part had most definitely mutated him into something very different. Then again, maybe our original perspective was not too far off the mark. I'll now tell you precisely what I mean by that.

The old man immediately surprised us by claiming that the horse's death was not the result of an accident or of the rigors of old age. Rather, he said, it was the diabolical work of something that he called the Wyrley Gang, a shadowy, local group dedicated to appeasing the ancient deities and earth gods of times past that it worshipped via the sacrifice of animals. This was absolutely great, we thought.

When one of us asked the old man how he knew this, he motioned us to move away from the foul-smelling body and sit on a nearby patch of thick, warm grass, which we all duly did. He then embarked upon a wild, macabre tale of infamous horse mutilations that had occurred decades earlier, but, astonishingly, only a little more than one-mile from Pelsall. It involved a man named George Edalji, as well as Sir Arthur Conan Doyle. It was a tale of dark and deadly proportions, one that my mates and I have never forgotten.

Royden—Not George Nor Jack—the Ripper

Just like Pelsall, the very nearby locale of Great Wyrley was once dominated by the mining industry, and its origins can also be traced back to the *Domesday Book*, where it was referenced under the name of Wereleia, a name derived from two Old English words "wir," meaning "bog," and "leah," which translates as "woodland clearing." Wyrley, too, was once wind-swept boggy moorland, just like north Pelsall. So, with that said, here is the old man's tale of the Wyrley Gang. [3]

The eldest of three children, George Ernest Thompson Edalji was born to parents Shapurji Edalji and Charlotte Stoneham in March 1876, and lived in Great Wyrley until his twenties. His father was of Indian descent, specifically a Parsi from Bombay, and his mother was born to Scottish parents. To the suspicious folk of Great Wyrley, the Edaljis were a mysterious bunch, best avoided at all costs. How could it be, asked some of the populace, in distinctly racist tones, that "an Asian could be a minister of a Christian church?" Indeed, George's father took on the role of vicar at Great Wyrley's St. Mark's Parish Church, which still stands to this very day. On top of that, after the family moved to the town, they began receiving a number of threatening and intimidating letters from an alleged group describing itself as the Wyrley Gang. That only made matters worse for the Edaljis. The family, therefore, was embroiled in controversy from its earliest years in Great Wyrley. And the situation soon got a great deal worse.

George Edalji was an intelligent soul who gravitated to law and became a solicitor working in Birmingham during the early 1900s. He also received a number of awards from the Law Society and even penned his very own book, *Railway Law for the Man in the Train*, which was "intended as a guide for the Travelling Public." But it was not his work in the field of law, nor his book that propelled George Edalji to the status of near-infamy all across the nation. It was something else. It was something shocking, something horrific, that ultimately caught the imagination and attention of the nation— and in later years, numerous devotees of Forteana.

In October 1903, Edalji was convicted of slashing and maiming a number of horses at the nearby Plant Pit Meadow. He was sentenced to seven years hard labor. Although Edalji vehemently protested his innocence throughout the course of his arrest, trial, and conviction, there was much talk that he had deliberately "sacrificed" the horses to ancient earth gods, although the evidence against Edalji was flimsy, to say the very least. Curiously, it emerged—perhaps as a result of the revelation in court that the Edalji clan had long been perceived by the locals as being very strange and best kept away from—that when the attacks were at their height, police immediately raced around to the Edalji residence to arrest George, rather than carry out an impartial investigation into the killings. Guilt on someone's part in the Edalji family, it seems, was already assumed, or had been decided upon, by the authorities.

The Chief Constable of the Staffordshire Police Force, who was responsible for coordinating the investigation, openly admitted that he believed "black men less than beasts," and concluded that Edalji was personally responsible for penning the anonymous letters that the family had previously received. All this without the benefit of any hard evidence that it was so, it must be said.

Edalji was eventually released from prison in 1906, but only after the efforts and pleas of R.D. Yelverton, who had previously worked as the Chief Justice in the Bahamas, and who was convinced there had been a distinct miscarriage of justice. Edalji was not pardoned, however, and he continued to be watched closely and secretly by local police for years. It was because of the apparent police prejudice and profiling that Sir Arthur Conan Doyle entered the controversy. Doyle spent eight months deeply immersed in the disturbing affair, an experience that he chronicled in his 1907 title, *The Story of Mr. George Edalji*, in which he concluded that Edalji was innocent of the late night slaughter. The real culprit, or one of them at the *very* least, Doyle forcefully suggested, may have been a local butcher's boy named Royden Sharp, an unsavory character who seemed to pop up regularly in the story, and in the direct vicinity of the mutilations, too.

When Doyle came to believe that Edalji was not the mastermind behind the horse mutilations, he sent the results of his findings to both the British Government's Home Office and the London-based *Daily Telegraph* newspaper. With publicity suddenly mounting, the Home Office agreed to appoint a committee to re-examine the case, which duly concluded that Edalji *had* been wrongly accused of horse-maiming after all. Even after this overturning, however, Edalji was never financially compensated for the three years he spent in prison, and Staffordshire Police still considered him guilty of writing those anonymous threatening letters to his own family.

Years later, however, a laborer named Enoch Knowles, who lived in the town of Wednesbury, confessed to having sent the Wyrley Gang letters over the course of what ultimately amounted to an astonishing three-decade period. As a result of his confession, the eccentric Knowles was arrested and convicted in 1934. George Edalji, meanwhile, who was never really able to successfully cast off the dark shadow of suspicion that had fallen upon him, died on June 17, 1953, from coronary thrombosis. If awful secrets he held, then they most certainly went with him to the grave.

That, essentially, was the story told to us, an enthralled gang of 12 and 13 year olds, who had suddenly been exposed to a fascinating series of events, packed with high-level shenanigans, mysterious attacks on animals, and claims of supernatural sacrifice to unholy deities that had all occurred barely spitting-distance from where we lived, albeit some 70 or so years earlier.

But that was not all. The old man of the moors told us that he had heard tales that the legend of the so-called Wyrley Gang had given birth to a very *real* Wyrley Gang, who were now, in the summer of 1977, operating in the area, and who were carrying on from where George Edalji or Royden Sharp—the jury was still very much out on the matter—had left off. The purpose of the newly formed Wyrley Gang, we were told, was to offer the unfortunate animals to the gods of old in return for riches and power. And, just maybe, the poor animal we had stumbled upon on the wilds of the North Common was evidence that the Wyrley Gang was operating under cover of darkness on the fringes of Pelsall. Wide-eyed and open-mouthed, all of us most certainly were. [4]

That was it. The old man stood up, and with his faithful hound in tow, bid us goodbye and went on his way. I recall that we saw him several times again that hot summer, always at a distance, but never failing to acknowledge us with a wave of his cane. Come the following summer, he was gone, but to where exactly, we never knew. And, by the summer holidays after that, childhood pursuits on pedal bikes had been replaced fully by music, girls, and part-time jobs.

From time to time, and despite its age, the story of George Edalji still surfaces within the pages of books and magazines, and still does the rounds in both Pelsall and Great Wyrley. There is, however, one particularly intriguing, yet very seldom discussed, aspect of the controversy, namely, its deep and undeniable links to cryptozoology and exotic animals.

A New Lead Surfaces

In November 2010, I received a transatlantic phone call from a man asking if "you were Nick Redfern, the author." I replied that, yes, I *was* Nick Redfern, the author—and, just for good measure, I added that I still *am* Nick Redfern, the author. The voice at the other end of the phone was that of a man named Jonathan Crossland, a descendent of the infamous Royden Sharp, who Sir Arthur Conan Doyle concluded played a key role in the 1903 horse-ripping events at Great Wyrley. Well, this was all very interesting. I asked Crossland what it was that had made him contact me. His answer was to the point.

In slightly whispered tones, Crossland said that he had a story of paramount importance to tell, which suggested neither George Edalji nor Royden Sharp were the culprits in the infamous attacks of yesteryear. Rather fantastically, Crossland's amazing tale pointed the finger of guilt at *culprits that weren't even human.* He suggested that strange beasts roaming the old neighborhood by night were the real attackers. This got me listening very intently.

Crossland was looking to tell his tale to someone who (a) knew the story of Edalji (he had seen a report I had written on the matter for Jon Downes' Center for Fortean Zoology a few years earlier), (b) who had researched animal mutilation cases, and (c) who was very familiar with the area where the attacks had taken place. I fit the bill on all three accounts. Since I was actually due to make a brief —*very* brief— return trip to England in March 2011, I decided to hook up with Crossland and hear what he had to say about old George and the Great Wyrley mutilations.

When it came to planning the location where we would meet up, Crossland asked me, in his posh, cultured tones: "I presume you keep a home in both England and America?" He presumed very wrong! I cannot even begin to tell you the number of people who, over the years, have assumed that just because I write books, then I must live in a huge mansion (or, as Crossland assumed, two), have a bulging bank-account, and drive a gleaming Ferrari or something similar. The truth is very different, as most souls who earn a living in the precarious world of freelance writing will only be too well aware.

So I explained to Crossland, "No, I do *not* have the luxury of having homes dotted all across the globe, and I'll be crashing out for five days at my dad's place on a blow-up mattress on his living room floor." So, if he wanted to meet up, it would have to be in Pelsall. This was fine with Crossland as, although he had long moved out of the area, he was pleased to return and meet up at a place—my dad's— that was barely a 10 minute drive from where the infamous attacks had occurred back in 1903. So, a date and a time were planned.

On a cold, wind-swept Saturday, I finally met Crossland, who turned out to be a tall, 70-something, highly flamboyant character who rather reminded me of the late Fortean author John Michell. Crossland was related to Royden Sharp via his father's side of the family, and his uncle had been married to a second cousin of Sharp's wife—or something along those lines; it all got a bit confusing, I have to admit. So, yes, the link was hardly first generation. I don't think we can even positively call it second generation. But, I figured that, at the end of the day, a link, no matter how distant and fragmentary, is still a link.

As we sat and dined on red wine and snacks of cheese and crackers in my dad's conservatory, and while a powerful wind battered its rain-soaked windows, Crossland told me of how he had devoured just about all the published books and papers on the Edalji affair (including mine for Jon Downes); had spent weeks digging into old newspaper reports on the events of 1903; had researched his family history in depth, and particularly so the life of Royden Sharp; and in the process had discovered something both fascinating and unusual. Namely, the aforementioned connection between the Great Wyrley attacks and strange creatures said to have been roaming the area by night at the very same time. I swear the grim weather proceeded to get even more torturous as Crossland laid out before me his admittedly extraordinary and macabre findings. [5]

Monstrous Mutilators

When the Great Wyrley horse-maiming was at its height, a number of very odd animal-based theories for the attacks *did* indeed surface amongst worried local folk, one being that the guilty party was a man disguised as a cow or a horse! Another suggested that the culprit was a great bird of prey or some other oversized winged beast (the Mothman or Owlman, maybe?), and a third mused upon the idea that the killer was some form of "malicious aviator," whatever the hell that meant. [6]

Then there were the strange revelations of George Edalji himself. He claimed to have been quietly told, by a close confidante who lived in the area, that the horse killings were the result of someone releasing into the area, late at night, a number of highly aggressive, wild boar. Supposedly, the notoriously bad tempered, thuggish beasts sought out the horses, committed their atrocious and bloodthirsty acts, and then, under cover of darkness, returned to the safety of their hidden lair, all at the bidding of their unknown master. Edalji admitted to not being particularly impressed by such a tale, but related it for what it was worth, or was not worth. And, of course, one has to wonder how someone would have the ability to train such wild animals, have them attack specific targets, and then convince them to repeatedly return home right afterwards, rather than enjoying their newfound freedom in the wilds of Staffordshire! [7]

Regardless of whether or not this story possessed even the modicum of merit, it is a fact that, today, wild boar most certainly *do* roam the depths of the very nearby Cannock Chase woods. In the summer of 2006, Andy Richardson, a journalist with the Walsall *Express & Star* newspaper, interviewed me. The subject of the interview was the research I was then undertaking for my 2008 book *There's Something in the Woods*. During the course of the interview,

I happened to mention to Andy that I had received scant details of a couple of sightings on the Cannock Chase of what sounded suspiciously like wild boar. Andy immediately expressed profound amazement, and he quickly proceeded to tell me how, some time previously when he had been working for Cannock's *Chase Post* newspaper, he had arrived at work one morning to be told by one of the receptionists that she had seen, on her way to the offices, "a big black pig run across the road in front of her." Andy told me that based on the woman's clear description it was quite obvious that what she had actually seen was indeed a large, adult, wild boar. [8]

There were still more animal-based stories and theories for the Edalji controversy. Crossland referred me to the work of Gordon Weaver, the author of the book *Conan Doyle and the Parson's Son: The George Edalji Case*, who noted of the horse maiming events that: "A Dudley man, claiming it was 'the work of an hypnotized ape,' left Great Wyrley in a huff after the Zoological Society refused to give him data on the behavior of the Simeon family of apes when under mesmeric influence." [9]

Just as is the case with the wild boar, the Cannock Chase, which is barely a couple of miles from Great Wyrley, is today a veritable hotbed of reports pertaining to sightings of large, unidentified apes. Some of them even border upon the likes of Bigfoot and the Abominable Snowman, as admittedly incredible as such a scenario most certainly sounds, and as I detailed in *There's Something in the Woods*. [10] But for the most notable exotic animal story that has a direct link to the George Edalji controversy, we have to turn our attentions to a local individual that Crossland believed was central to the story of what really happened on those cold, dark and disturbing nights in Great Wyrley back at the turn of the 20th century, a man named Dr. John Kerr Butter.

The Doctor's Secrets

More than a century ago, Dr. Butter kept what could easily be described as a menagerie of wild and exotic animals in his backyard, which stood on the grounds of what is today Cannock's Wolverhampton Road Police Station, barely a stone's throw from Great Wyrley and the terrible carnage of 1903. Butter's neighbors were regularly confronted by a wild assortment of animals craning their necks over his garden fence, including, astonishingly enough, a fully grown giraffe! Records reveal that Butter had personally raised and tamed a wild cat—specifically an ocelot—a feat that was then considered pretty much impossible by the zoological elite of the day, and something that earned the doctor the lofty distinction of being made a Fellow of the Royal Zoological Society. And, somewhat amusingly, patients at Dr. Butter's office would often find themselves sitting in the waiting room next to his favorite monkey, Antony, who had practically turned Butter's practice into a home from home. [11]

There is also the interesting fact that, in March 1892, the good doctor was on-hand to provide emergency medical treatment when an African lion-tamer named Delhi Montarno was mauled by three Russian bears and a hyena "during a performance of wild beasts" in the town of Cannock. The show was put on by a famous traveling organization called Wombwell & Baileys Menagerie and Circus, the brainchild of a man named George Wombwell. Unfortunately, and despite Dr. Butter's very best efforts to save him, Montarno was so severely injured that he died within 20 minutes of the vicious onslaught. [12]

Dr. Butter's links to exotic animals didn't end there. He amassed a large collection of artifacts in his laboratory, including everything from bear skins to alligator jaws that had been made into pen-and-ink stands, as well as jars of carefully preserved animal organs. The populace of Cannock also held Butter in very high regard. For example, when the Second Boer War broke out in 1899, the doctor immediately elected to do his duty for his country, and on the day of his departure for the war-torn South African battlefield, "nearly the whole town gathered to see him off," according to the *Chase Post* newspaper. [13]

Local historian Dave Battersby said: "He was the recognized doctor in the town and was very well known many years after his death. He obviously did a lot of good for a lot of people. He trained people in first-aid." The doctor did indeed, and he also established the very first ambulance service to operate across the Cannock Chase. But there was a far more significant development still to come. With the outbreak of the First World War in 1914, food supplies in the Cannock area dwindled dramatically, and Dr. Butter was unfortunately forced to let virtually all his animals go. [14]

No one seemed to know what happened to the doctor's huge collection of creatures. But since there have not been any reports of giraffes running wild in the woods of the Cannock Chase, it seems very safe to assume that this particular beast was successfully re-housed somewhere else. As for the rest of the menagerie, Dave Battersby added that: "It's likely they were given to other collectors or to zoos. The moving of animals wouldn't be newsworthy at the time and so archives won't tell us much about where the animals went." [15]

Certainly, there is still no available evidence to suggest that the creatures had been donated to other zoos. But there is no evidence to suggest that the animals were put to sleep, either. They had just vanished completely and utterly, unless the good doctor decided that the wisest approach to solving the problem was to clandestinely release his much loved animals into the wilds of Staffordshire late one night when everyone else was asleep and tucked up in their beds.

If he had done so, and if several such animals had subsequently successfully bred, then that would very possibly go some significant way towards possibly explaining the presence of large, wild cats on the Cannock Chase, and throughout the rest of Staffordshire today. And encounters with Antony's offspring, and their offspring, might help explain a few of the truly baffling sightings of small monkey-like animals throughout Staffordshire and the nearby woods, albeit certainly not their larger cousins.

But there is something else too, as Crossland told me, and which I was able to confirm as 100 percent fact: Dr. John Kerr Butter played a key and integral role in the George Edalji affair. At the height of the horse attacks in Great Wyrley, the doctor was retained by Staffordshire Police to analyze Edalji's clothing, primarily for any evidence of horse hair, something that, if confirmed, might very well have proved the man's guilt. The doctor also provided evidence and testimony during the course of Edalji's trial, and ultimately became a central character in the overall saga. [16]

When Crossland related this to me, I finally realized where he was going with the winding story. Crossland believed that, back in 1903, some of the good doctor's animals had escaped from their confines—maybe even including an ocelot or two—and *they* were actually the culprits, *not* Edalji, and not even Conan Doyle's primary suspect, Royden Sharp. Crossland further believed that as the local police and the populace were hardly on good terms with the Edalji clan, blaming the horse attacks on Edalji would have been an extremely good way to possibly encourage the family to leave the area. Crossland also concluded that Dr. Butter had a very solid reason for wanting the attacker to be perceived as a person rather than an animal: it would have diverted attention away from all talk that perhaps his own predatory beasts had escaped and carried out the grisly attacks.

"What are you going to do with this story?" I then asked Crossland.

"Nothing," was his reply, before suddenly standing up, turning on his heels, heading out into the dark and rainy afternoon, and hitting the roads in his old black Jaguar. "It's all yours to tell now." And so, tell Crossland's story I have. True or not, it serves to demonstrate that this case, now fast approaching its 110th anniversary, simply refuses to roll over and die, unlike all those unfortunate horses back in 1903. [17]

A Strange Anniversary

There are several other tangential issues worth noting in relation to this curious affair. First, exactly 100 years after the Great Wyrley horse ripping activities of 1903 occurred, another cryptozoological mystery reared its ugly head barely a few hundred yards from where the Edalji family lived all those decades earlier. During the summer of 2003, all hell broke loose when sightings began of a strange creature, or creatures, said to inhabit a sizeable body of water called Roman View Pond, situated barely spitting distance from the old Edalji residence. Hysterical rumors spread around the town of Cannock to the effect that a giant, marauding crocodile was on the loose in Roman View Pond.

Local police, representatives of the Royal Society for the Prevention of Cruelty to Animals (RSPCA), and the nation's media all quickly descended upon the scene, as they valiantly sought to ascertain the truth about what, at a local level, fast became known to one and all as the "Cannock Nessie." What a name. What a surprise. The facts, however, were rather more sober and down to earth than the newspapers might have wished. As Jon Downes and

Richard Freeman demonstrated to practically everyone's satisfaction when they personally visited the area at the height of the hysteria, the "beast," as the more sensationalistic elements of the press tirelessly insisted on calling it, was likely nothing stranger than a three-foot-long Spectacled Caiman, a crocodilian reptile found throughout much of Central and South America.

Jon and Richard concluded that the unfortunate creature had probably been housed locally by an unknown exotic pet-keeper, until it grew to a point where it became completely unmanageable, and was then unceremoniously dumped in the pond late one night and under the protective cover of darkness. Almost certainly, Jon came to believe, the Caiman would not survive the harsh fall and winter months that were destined to follow. And, sure enough, as the English weather changed for the worse, sightings of the mysterious beast came to an abrupt end. To this day, Jon is convinced that the bones of the crocodilian lay buried deep in the muddy floor of Roman View Pond. And he's almost certainly correct.

But the fact that the beast had surfaced right in the same area and the same time that the Edalji case was once again big news (in terms of its 100th anniversary "celebrations") certainly added yet another cryptozoological veneer to the seemingly never ending saga. [18]

Making Britain Monstrous

While he and Richard Freeman were investigating the affair of the beast of Roman View Pond, Jon Downes recorded something else that was decidedly odd. "We found ourselves in the middle of Cannock Chase," he noted, "and deep in conversation with the local wildlife officers who told us that koi had also been turning up in isolated ponds across Cannock Chase, as well. It seems as if there is some kind of strange, Piscine Johnny Appleseed at work, doing his best to stock of the waterways of the West Midlands with these large, ornamental fish."

And, six years later, in 2009, it seems that someone was yet again up to their old, nighttime tricks, and once more anonymously dumping exotic creatures in a certain body of water around the town of Cannock. On this occasion, however, the scene of all the action was not Roman View Pond but a small, three-meter-deep pool that is hidden in a corner of the Brickworks Nature Reserve at Wimblebury, which is practically no distance at all from the heart of the Cannock Chase or prime Edalji territory.

As the *Chase Post* newspaper humorously noted at the time, up until recently "the only things lurking in the murky waters were six bicycles, a shopping trolley and scaffolding poles." But all that changed in 2009. Cannock Chase Council officials, concerned about vegetation dying, made a startling discovery, said the *Post*, adding that amongst the usual debris and rubbish, "there were fish in the water, lots of fish—20,000, to be precise. Even more baffling, there were not just native species; as well as roach and perch, ornamental varieties such as brown goldfish and koi carp were found." [19]

So, you may ask: where am I going with all this? Well, in July 2010, I received a phone call from a man named Terry Baxter, who lives in Birmingham, England, and who had seen an article I had written some time ago on the Birmingham eel encounters of the 1980s described in Chapter Three of this book. Terry had an intriguing theory to explain why people were, and still are, seemingly dumping exotic animals in the waters all across the West Midlands and Staffordshire. He didn't doubt that such actions were overwhelmingly reckless, however, and I fully agreed with him. While letting such creatures loose in deep ponds on a nice sunny day during a hot English summer might seem, for some, like a good idea at the time, when autumn and winter arrive, the creatures are unlikely to survive for very long at all, which is precisely why the "Cannock Nessie" was so active in the summer of 2003, but summarily vanished forever as the good old English weather got worse and colder.

But Terry was not of the opinion that ignorant, stupid people were simply dumping these beasts because they had grown too large and vicious to handle. This wasn't the work of inexperienced owners simply getting rid of their increasingly aggressive pets, he believed. Rather, Terry claimed second-hand knowledge of a group in the Midlands that was "very Fortean" in its nature, beliefs and pursuits. He felt that the group was trying, albeit in a somewhat unwise and skewed way, to "make Britain mysterious again."

Somewhat puzzled, I asked Terry to clarify exactly what he meant by that, and he replied that, in centuries past, Britain was packed with legends of strange and savage beasts of all amazing manner: dragons, griffins, giant worms, and much more. But that today, he said, "All we've got left are big cats, and even Nessie has gone off the radar." Well, I wouldn't say it's quite that black and white and simplistic, but he did have a point. So, according to "certain information" Terry claimed to have acquired, there were—and still are—people in the West Midlands and Staffordshire trying to turn back the clocks on the sterile concrete jungle, and create modern day mysteries of a "water-monster" variety, specifically by introducing exotic animals to certain parts of the British Isles.

Terry explained the situation, and the actions of the group, like this: "They want to see legends developing of the 'Great Serpent of Cannock,' or the 'Giant Fish of Birmingham,' really so that the old stories and legends will live again and England will be magical and mysterious again." Whether Terry was right or not was a moot point. But there's no doubt at all that there had indeed been regular dumping of exotic animals in the waters around Cannock and Great Wyrley for years. I don't support such actions at all, nor do I think it's a good idea to populate Britain's waters with exotic animals, chiefly because many of them cannot cope with the rigors of the British weather, and they soon die. But, as a theory, I couldn't rule out the possibility that this is precisely what was, and maybe still is, going on and why. [20]

A Movie and a Monster

Moving on, but still on matters of an Edalji and Great Wyrley nature, renowned cryptozoologist Loren Coleman noted that the classic 1967 Hammer film *Five Million Years to Earth* (originally titled *Quatermass and the Pit*) tells of a new excavation of the London Underground in an area called Hobbs End, the result of which is the discovery of a spaceship built by long-dead aliens.

Coleman said: "The scientists involved in the unraveling of this drama soon discover this part of London on Hobbs Lane has a long history of poltergeist, haunting, and apparition activities. One keen young researcher discovers an old street sign near the diggings, and she notes the spelling is 'Hob's Lane,' not 'Hobbs Lane.' 'Hob,' it turns out, is another name for 'devil,' or the 'Devil,' if you prefer. Even the descriptive verb 'hobble' refers to the word's origins, as the classic view of the Devil shows cloven hooves." [21]

Somewhat incredibly, it's worth pointing out that very close to what was once prime George Edalji and Royden Sharp territory there is an old road called…Hobble End Lane. Was the name merely there by chance? Or, as in *Five Million Years to Earth*, had there been devilish activity afoot in the area for years? If so, did it prompt the people of the area to adopt an equally devilish name for their old and mysterious lane? Given that some Great Wyrley folk believed there was a sacrificial aspect to the horse mutilations, perhaps such a possibility should be given some careful consideration, rather than being summarily dismissed out of hand.

We may never truly know if the rumors of cryptozoological, occult, and devil-like links to the George Edalji case have any bearing upon the real nature and origin of the attacks on the unfortunate horses that Edalji was found guilty of maiming. To find, however, that one of the key players in the affair possessed his very own Ocelot (and which ultimately went missing), that wild and aggressive boar were on the loose only a few miles away (and still are), and that even back in the old days of Edalji there was dark talk of "apes" roaming the area, led me to wonder if there might be certain Fortean and cryptozoological aspects to the case that have, thus far, either been overwhelmingly ignored, or that remain manifestly unappreciated by those looking for a more conventional explanation to this still-baffling mystery. Just maybe, one day, the theories of Jonathan Crossland will prove to be nothing less than hard, quite amazing, facts.

Chapter 15
Dead Heads, Demons, and a Damned Dam

"Did you hear *that?*"

Bigfoot in the Park

Midway through May 2011, I was asked to speak at a conference that would be held in McGee Creek State Park, Oklahoma, in September called the Cryptid Fest. Oklahoma is, for those who may not be aware, prime Bigfoot territory, and sure enough the conference proved quite memorable, chiefly because there were those at the event who actually claimed to have seen several Bigfoot—right at the site of the outdoor event, at 3:00 p.m. in the afternoon, and hiding behind trees and spying upon the audience and speakers, no less! [1]

Here is what happened. In attendance at the conference was a crew from the local Fox News channel, who were eager and anxious to put together a small segment on the Cryptid Fest for the Saturday night news and the good folk of Oklahoma. It so transpires that while the TV team was running around, setting up cameras, and arranging interviews word started to quietly but quickly circulate that some of the people in attendance had found a curious area of flattened grass only a few hundred feet from where the gig was being held. Not only that, but near the very same site large, humanoid footprints were in evidence, too. And, get this: There had been brief and tantalizing sightings of massive, dark figures using the trees as cover to spy on what was afoot, before finally retreating into the denser parts of the woods. The story got even more jaw-dropping: People had also seen what looked like an adult male and female, as well as a juvenile Bigfoot, and had even heard the beasts mimicking the cries of crows. How they knew the sounds weren't of *real* crows was never really explained. And, to top it all off, there was even a fleeting sighting of a large, tan-colored, four-legged creature racing through the woods in the very same locale where the Bigfoot family was seen. Exactly what the hell *that* latter critter might have been, I have no idea at all.

Clearly overjoyed by such great (or suspicious) timing on the part of Bigfoot and family, Fox News quickly shot footage of the area, launched into a hastily planned question and answer session with the witnesses, and also chatted with Ken Gerhard and I as we made our way towards the action. Yes, there *was* a flattened area of ground. And there was also what did look like footprints with clearly defined toes in evidence. As for the legendary monsters themselves, the camera crew recorded the witnesses as saying precisely what you would expect them to say under such circumstances: They saw something big, hairy, and manlike: Bigfoot. [2]

The claimed events not only provoked a fair degree of interest, they also inevitably ensured a considerable amount of eye rolling. But this curious event, however, certainly set the scene for what was to come after the gig was over, and dinner and beer had been eagerly devoured, namely a late night trek around the forest in search of the beast, or beasts, in question.

Seeking Sasquatch by Moonlight
There were 12 of us who chose to take part in the moonlit adventures, and we all paired-up, just in case any of us got separated and lost, which given the territory and the darkness, would not have been impossible and certainly not a good thing. I was paired-up with Chase Kloetzke, an all-round adventurer and devotee of the unexplained. The plan was for Ken to lead the way into the dense woods and demonstrate to people the down-to-earth things to look out for, as well as the not so down-to-earth ones, while on a nighttime quest for Bigfoot. And Ken did a fantastic job. One of the most significant things he did, as we made our careful way through the incredibly thick and near never ending trees, was to mimic a certain action of Bigfoot that has been recorded on countless occasions: tree-knocking, as it has become known in Sasquatch-seeking circles. [3]

For reasons not entirely understood, when people are out in the woods, Bigfoot very often displays an unsettling propensity for repeatedly banging hard on tree trunks, sometimes violently so. Maybe it's to scare people away from what it perceives as its territory. Well, if that is the case, it has certainly worked on a number of occasions. So Ken found a good sized branch and proceeded to whack a few trees as hard as he could, just to see if anything followed. This coincided with another of the team-members mimicking the high-pitched crying howl that has, at times, been attributed to Bigfoot. If something large and monstrous was around, right now was the time for it to tell us. And maybe it did exactly that. [4]

Just around the time of the knocking and the mimicked howling, we all briefly heard what sounded like a strange, animalistic cry, very nearby. It even provoked what seemed to be a return knocking, too. And the call was definitely not of the type that one would attribute to a wild animal of a known variety. I heard someone shout, nearby, in concerned fashion: "Did you hear *that*?" Yes, we did, all of us. Not surprisingly, everyone wanted to push further and deeper, which is precisely what happened for a while. But if Bigfoot was around, it chose to bring the night's proceedings to a close soon thereafter. After that tantalizing piece of terrorizing, we heard no more. It was, however, a fitting end to a day and night filled with outright beastly bizarreness.

My September 2010 investigations were not quite over, however. There was yet another unknown animal to deal with, and this one was far closer to home than the monsters of Oklahoma's McGee Creek State Park. It had actually all begun one month before the Cryptid Fest, but increased dramatically in the weeks that followed my trek around the woods of Oklahoma.

Heads Are Going to Roll
Something undeniably weird started to happen in my backyard in late August 2011. While out watering the grass one day, I stumbled upon the freshly dead body of a decapitated mole in the grass, which I thought was kind of odd, but didn't give it much thought at the time. Ken Gerhard saw the mauled and mutilated creature when he came to visit shortly afterwards and concurred with me that some local predator had undeniably killed the mole. Of what specific variety was the big question, of course. Things didn't end there, however. About two weeks later, I found a large, skinned bone on the lawn. From what kind of animal it came, I did not know, but it had been picked entirely clean of meat. And there was much worse to come.

I had spent the morning of September 24 getting everything ready for a drive down to Austin, Texas, where I was due to lecture that evening for S. Miles Lewis' Anomaly Archives group. After I finished getting all of my lecture material together, and duly mapped the drive to the location, I went to sit outside for an hour so, before it was time for me to hit the highway south for a handful of hours and a fistful of dollars. Only a couple of minutes after, I noticed something shocking: the torn off, or bitten off, head of a possum was sitting, oddly upright, on the small paved area on which my grill sat. I stared, dumbfounded, for a few seconds, then I got up, walked over, and had a close look at it. There was no doubting it: the unknown predator that had made a meal of something's bones, and torn the head off a mole, was surely back.

I cannot be sure what kind of beast chose the yard as its hunting ground, but what I can say for certain is that twice in the year leading up to the attacks I saw a coyote in the street directly outside my house. The first time was in June 2010, the very night when I came back from my mom's funeral in England. On the second occasion, with my dad in attendance, I saw it late at night during a very violent thunderstorm in late May 2011, when once again it was charging along the road outside of my home.

Not everyone I spoke to was convinced that the beast was a coyote, however. When the attacks were at their height, I had an email exchange with England-based big cat expert Neil Arnold. In reference to certain unresolved animal killings in his home county of Kent that he believed to be the work of big and wild cats, Neil wrote to me: "I've been investigating several cases of fox and domestic cat heads turning up. Maybe worth having a look round your field—scratch marks on the fence? Tufts of fur? The possum was probably killed in your garden, blood lapped up, body taken over fence." [5]

In response to Neil's email, I wrote: "Cheers for the advice and info!" I added that, on two occasions, I had noticed "a very strong smell of animal urine in the garden, as if it has been marking its territory…It wouldn't be hard for something to get on [the] roof, as there are trees all around it that something could jump from." [6]

To which Neil replied: "I'm currently investigating two cases locally of large cats being seen on the roof areas of bungalows! A perfect area for a cat to sit up and watch over the landscape. Keep me updated. Also, might be worth looking around in the trees." Plus, although I live in a city, right behind the house is a huge stretch of wild, long-grassed field that extends for hundreds of feet square and which would be the ideal place for a savage predator to hide out. [7]

Even though there was an undoubted coyote presence in the area, there was another reason, beyond those suggested by Neil that made me think a coyote was not the real culprit after all. The fence was relatively new, extended to a height of nearly eight-feet, and displayed no evidence of anything having burrowed under it. So if a coyote was the cause of the head-severing episode, it would have had to have carried away the body of a full-grown possum in its mouth and then scaled an eight-foot-high fence in the process. Not a totally impossible scenario, but many people I spoke with were very doubtful that a coyote could have scaled such a high fence with its mouth full of a dead possum. They, too, suggested an exotic cat of some unknown type.

But there was another possibility that crossed my mind. It was far from being a positive possibility, and it had nothing to do with wild animals on the loose. Since the head of the possum seemed to have been pretty much sliced off, was sitting absolutely upright when I noticed it, and had seemingly been positioned in a place where I was pretty much guaranteed to see it from the very outset, I wondered if this was somehow linked to the activities of the Taigheirm. Doubtful, yes, but bear with me.

Throughout late 2010 and most of 2011, I had been digging deep into the saga of ritual-based cat mutilations and alleged Taigheirm activities in the nearby city of Dallas. Try as I might, I could not get out of my mind the theory that Taigheirm operatives might have elected to send me a warning, in the form of the severed, carefully placed possum head, to keep my nose out of something that, from their perspective, did not concern me.

Had dedicated occultists skulked around my yard in the dead of night? Was this their own unique equivalent of the Mafia placing a horse's head in someone's bed as a dire warning, as most famously portrayed in Francis Ford Coppola's 1972 movie, *The Godfather*? It was a disturbing thought. By January 2012, the weird killings of animals in the yard had finally stopped; my research into a potential Taigheirm link to Dallas, however, has not—nor will it. But I still keep a careful lookout for further remains, and for any evidence of dark-cloaked disciples of the Taigheirm creeping about and leaving macabre messages. The chaos and carnage in the Redfern backyard was very far from over, however. [8]

Thunderstruck!

On the night of October 17, 2011, the city of Arlington was hit by a thunderstorm of near-apocalyptic proportions. For hours that night, pounding wind, deluge-like rain, and wild lightning filled the skies, pummeling just about everything in sight. As the witching hour loomed, and the weather boomed, I was watching for the umpteenth time my all-time favorite movie, *Night of the Demon*, a 1957 production starring Dana Andrews, which is based on the classic M.R. James story, *The Casting of the Runes*. Suddenly, out of the blue, a spectacular, explosion-like rumble shook the house and sent the electricity into a wild, flickering frenzy. And, whatever had happened, it had taken place in the backyard, that increasingly strange locale dominated by beheaded animals, a discarded bone, and in earlier times, black helicopters above, and a dead frog sitting atop my very own Stonehenge.

I flung opened the door to a scene of utter carnage. The mighty oak tree that sits just outside the window of the second bedroom had taken a full lightning strike, which had brought down two of its biggest and highest positioned branches – each about 12 feet long and each more than a foot thick. A multitude of smaller branches had also come crashing to the ground in the process. Worse still, the two main branches had fallen on the fence that separates the house from that of my neighbor, causing a fair degree of damage to five or six fence posts. The fence had only been installed a year earlier. Bollocks. With the wind howling, the rain pouring, and the skies flashing chaotically, there was very little I could do until morning came, so I retired to bed, fuming and stewing.

One thought kept crossing my mind. Just 20 or so minutes before the branch-shattering strike occurred, I had watched a memorable scene in the *Night of the Demon* in which occultist Julian Carswell, brilliantly played by Irish actor Niall MacGinnis, uses devilish powers to conjure up…a wild storm that culminates in a bolt of lightning bringing down a large tree limb on his property.

The following morning, I opened the door to take a good look at the scene of destruction. What an unholy mess, I thought. I quickly arranged to get a tree-cutter over to get rid of the branches, followed by a local handyman who took care of the fence repairs. By late afternoon, no one would have known of the previous night's calamities. But while the remains of the branches were being cut up and carted away by the tree-cutter, my pool cleaner came along, and remarked that—since this was now the third tree in the yard that had suffered at the hands of Mother Nature in just such a fashion, yes, the *third*—"it's like you have a demon in the yard!" I almost did a double take when she uttered those words. Given everything that had gone on in the yard since I moved in the house during the summer of 2008, I could not entirely dismiss the possibility that the previous evening really had been a genuine night of the demon. [9]

The Gate of the Devil

At his birth in Los Angeles on October 2, 1914, one Jack Parsons was given the unusual name of Marvel Whiteside Parsons and had a truly extraordinary life. An undoubted genius, he indirectly led NASA to send the Apollo astronauts to the Moon in 1969. Moreover, the Aerojet Corporation, which Parsons founded, produced solid-fuel rocket boosters for the Space Shuttle that are based on Parsons' very own, decades-old innovations. For Parsons' personal accomplishments, a large crater on the far side of the Moon was named in his honor, and each year on Halloween, NASA's Jet Propulsion Laboratory holds an open-house memorial, known as "Nativity Day," replete with mannequins of Jack Parsons and his early JPL cohorts. Within the aerospace and astronautic communities, there is a longstanding joke that JPL actually stands for "Jack Parsons Laboratory" or "Jack Parsons Lives."

Parsons, who is still revered and honored by senior figures within the U.S. space program, was an admitted occultist, a follower of the "Great Beast" himself, Aleister Crowley, and someone who topped even Crowley himself by engaging in bestiality with the family dog and sexual relations with his own mother, perhaps at the same time, no less. Moreover, before each rocket test, to ensure a successful flight, Parsons would undertake a complicated ritual to try and invoke the Greek god, Pan.

It was perhaps inevitable that his path would eventually cross with that of Aleister Crowley. In 1942, after the two had become acquainted as a result of their like-minds and pursuits, Crowley chose Parsons to lead the Agape Lodge of the Thelemic Ordo Templi Orientis (O.T.O.) in California, after Crowley expelled Wilfred Smith from the position. The devoted Parsons eagerly practiced Aleister Crowley's Thelemic Rituals, the goal of which was the creation of a new breed of human being, which, if the ritual proved successful, would lead to the destruction of Christianity. Meanwhile, during the same timeframe, and within the confines of his Pasadena mansion, dubbed "The Parsonage," the handsome Parsons held parties for friends and colleagues in the field of science fiction. Indeed, writers Robert Heinlein, Jack Williamson, Anthony Boucher, and Ray Bradbury were all regular visitors to Parsons' home. So Parsons was a highly interesting character, who moved in intriguing circles filled with powerful and influential players.

Much of Parsons' and the JPL's initial rocket research in this period was undertaken at the Devil's Gate Dam in Pasadena, California. Interestingly, the JPL was itself established at this very locale in 1930 by the California Institute of Technology. The dam had been constructed a decade earlier by engineers from the Los Angeles County Flood Control District and took its title from Devil's Gate Gorge, a rocky out-cropping that eerily resembles a demonic face and which is located in a narrow canyon of the Arroyo Seco, which is a riverbed that extends from the San Gabriel into the Los Angeles basin. Some say that the demonic face is merely a classic case of pareidolia, the process by which the human brain can interpret random imagery as having some meaning or significance, a classic example being the way in which, at one time or another, most of us have seen faces in clouds. But is that really all that is behind the satanic face of the old dam? Maybe not. [10]

A Demon at the Dam

In late 2010, probably the most controversial book I have ever written was published. *Final Events* told the unsettling story of a think-tank-style group in the U.S. Government that addressed the UFO phenomenon at a secret level for more than half a century. The members came to believe that UFOs, rather than having extraterrestrial origins, were actually satanic in nature. And I do mean that literally. Fire, brimstone, the Devil, and a malignant deception in which coldhearted demons, masquerading as black eyed, diminutive aliens, were working to an agenda to provoke worldwide Armageddon and the enslavement of everyone's souls.

As so often happens whenever I have a new book out, people who read it, and who feel they have something to say about its contents, contact me. One of those who did just that after the publication of *Final Events* was a Pasadena, California, man named Bob Jessup who had an amazing story to relate concerning Devil's Gate Dam, a brief history of which I included in the book in telling the entertainingly bizarre story and history of Jack Parsons.

Jessup lived not too far from Devil's Gate Dam and claimed to have seen a terrifying beast at the foot of Devil's Gate Gorge only a few nights after reading *Final Events*. This almost sounded too good to be true, even by my standards. But I listened carefully to what Jessup had to say. With its surrounding and nearby hills, dense woodland, and winding pathways, Devil's Gate Gorge is an ideal place for hikers and horse-riders to hang out and get some exercise. Each weekday afternoon, after work, Jessup would walk his dog, Miles, for an hour or so around the wooded paths, while taking in the pleasant scenery. But what Jessup wanted to tell me was not pleasant.

On a cold, late afternoon in January 2011, Jessup was nearing Devil's Gate Gorge when he heard an ear-splitting screech that he said was like a combination of the shrill cry of a fox and someone dragging their fingernails across a chalkboard. It was extremely loud, very puzzling, and seemed to be coming from somewhere above him. Jessup looked around, first to the trees, then to the sloping pathway that one has to take from the dam down to the base of the gorge. No luck. It was when he looked closer at the gorge itself, and saw a milk-white colored, skinny, humanoid creature sporting a large pair of equally white bat-type wings, scaling the gorge, just like, in Jessup's very own words, "Spiderman climbing a building, or a big grasshopper." Jessup could only stand and stare in awe and fear as the creature turned and glared directly at him, issued another ear-splitting scream, and "hopped and jumped and leapt away over the top [of the gorge]." Jessup did not wait around to see if the winged monstrosity elected to return.

I spent about 45 minutes on the phone interviewing Jessup, who came across as lucid but puzzled, and not to mention significantly worried by the encounter. [11]

Of Death and Disappearance

The occult rituals of Jack Parsons and Bob Jessup's account aside, certainly the most disturbing thing about Devil's Gate Dam and Devils' Gate Gorge were the tragic deaths and disappearances of a number of children in the area back in the 1950s. In August of 1956, Donald Lee Baker, 13, and Brenda Howell, 11, vanished while riding their bicycles on land directly behind the dam. Both bicycles and Brenda's jacket were later found nearby. The children, unfortunately, were not. Then, in March 1957, an 8-year-old boy named Tommy Bowman seemingly vanished into the middle of nowhere while hiking around the gorge with his family. One minute, little Tommy was there; the next he was gone. Three years later, a young boy named Bruce Kremen vanished under mysterious circumstances in the same area.

As for Donald and Brenda, their disappearances were finally solved. A deranged serial killer named Mack Ray Edwards confessed to having killed them and a number of others, possibly as many as eighteen, between 1953 and 1970. Edwards' only good act in life was that he hung himself one day before Halloween in 1971, while doing time for his crimes in San Quentin State Prison. The cases of Tommy Bowman and Bruce Kremen remain unresolved, although fingers of suspicion certainly pointed in Edwards' direction.

Yet more tragedy and death has dominated this bleak area. Pasadena is also home to the Colorado Street Bridge, which just happens to cross over the Arroyo Seco bed. Locally, the large construction has a very different name: Suicide Bridge. Its nickname is very apt as the number of distressed people who have now thrown themselves off the bridge to their deaths since its construction in 1912 is now well into three figures.

Some might very well disagree, but it seemed to me that an atmosphere of negativity and evil had enveloped Devil's Gate Dam. Out of its darkness has come a serial killer, a winged demon, a famous occultist without whose work NASA would likely never have been founded, and an overwhelming number of suicides. Since many of the suicides predated Jack Parsons' presence at the area, we cannot lay the blame on his ritualistic ceremonies and his deep ties to the work of Aleister Crowley. But one cannot deny the possibility that

Parsons' actions may have succeeded in amplifying an already existing air of menace and negativity that already enveloped the devilish dam, for reasons presently unknown. With Bob Jessup's account in hand, the presence and actions of Jack Parsons carefully studied, and data on that spate of tragic deaths and mysterious disappearances now digested, I knew there was one thing more I needed to do. I had to check out the area for myself. [12]

A Gig, the Gorge, and Greg

In mid-2011 I was invited to do a workshop-style presentation on my research into the Men in Black mystery for the Los Angeles-based Conscious Life Expo conference on the first weekend in October. I always enjoy traveling to L.A. because, more often than not, it gives me the opportunity to see Greg Bishop and his wife, Sigrid. And after my Saturday night lecture, we arranged to hang out on Sunday afternoon.

Greg wanted to drive me around some of the weirder, Fortean parts of L.A. So we first stopped at the headquarters of the contactee-based Aetherius Society, then after lunch we took in the old building in which certain scenes from *Blade Runner* were filmed, and finally we ended up at Devil's Gate Dam. It was actually Greg's idea to check out the dam.

So I was here: at the gate of the Devil, the home to an albino-like winged fiend of the night (or of the late afternoon, in Bob Jessup's case). Greg parked the car, and we strolled along for a couple of hundred yards to a steep, downwards winding dusty path. It quickly led us out of the concrete surroundings of Pasadena and into the wild woods, dense trees, snaking waters, and large, looming hills. As we negotiated the rapidly changing landscape, it was hard not to muse upon the deeply unhappy history of the area. And, like all locales steeped in misery, death, and mystery, Devil's Gate Dam was saturated by that hard to define feeling of uneasiness that pervades so many such places. Finally, we reached the base of the dam and continued along the tree-shrouded track to our final quarry: Devil's Gate Gorge itself.

There was no winged fiend to be seen, and the ghost of Jack Parsons failed to manifest before us. But the afternoon was not without significance. Below the old Devil-like rock face is a long tunnel, the entrance to which is usually covered with bars, chains, and a large lock to prevent access to its depths. Fortunately for us, however, the lock was still in evidence, but it was open, and the chains holding it together were gone. So there was only one option available to us: we carefully squeezed our way through the gateway and began to walk through the dark old tunnel, wondering what we might find ahead of us. Or, perhaps, what might very well find us.

Stale, freezing, dank, and damp, the tunnel was hardly the most inviting of locales to hang out in on a Sunday afternoon in California. But I guess it could be argued that it was all quite appropriate for what was to come next. Although I said nothing to Greg about it at the time, I mentally focused upon the image of Bob Jessup's winged monstrosity, called it forth, and demanded it put in an appearance—either for us, right now, or for the people of Pasadena at a time when the demon itself saw fit. A reckless act, some might say, but maybe, one day, the beast will take note of my underground actions and return to Pasadena's devilish dam. I sincerely hope I am there when, and if, it chooses to do so. With the deed done, Greg and I left the dark tunnel behind, returned to the glare of the Californian afternoon, and hit the road. As we did so, I looked back at the dam one last time. You know, just in case.

Conclusions

From the beginning of 2009 to the end of 2011, my path crossed many a monstrous tale and curious experience. The stories collected and examined in that period clearly reinforced for me the idea that strange creatures most certainly are among us. Pursuing such things is not, and never has been, a waste of time. But while a very few of these cases did seem to suggest the presence of real, flesh and blood animals, most were far less easy to explain in down-to-earth terms.

Their behavior, their uncanny ability to always avoid capture, and, of course, the fact that in many cases the beasts in question were not stumbled upon but, rather, were deliberately conjured, or invoked, by infernal rite—whether in Dallas, Texas, in the woods of England's Cannock Chase, within the bleak valleys of Wales, or amid the old island communities of Scotland—is a clear indication that all is most certainly not what it seems to be in what passes for monster-hunting territory. Existence is one thing. The true nature of that existence is quite clearly yet another.

And on a significantly different topic, the stories and discoveries concerning the Flatwoods Monster of 1952, and the Houston Batman of the following year, suggest that some perceived monsters may actually be the ingenious creations of psychological warfare planners and manipulators buried deep within the the Pentagon and the CIA.

So what does all of this mean for cryptozoology? Well, as I noted at the beginning of this book, that very much depends upon how open those interested in such phenomena are to the notion that at least some wholly elusive cryptids have less to do with the physical, natural plane than they do with something much more mystifying. Belief is a powerful tool and an equally powerful influence. And convincing the "flesh and blood" cryptozoologists that strictly using scientific methods to prove the existence of Bigfoot, Ogopogo, or Nessie might actually be as useless as trying to explain the technology behind television to an ancient Egyptian is something that whole swathes of the cryptozoological community simply do not want to hear.

But I never meant to *convince* you of any particular theory, idea, or notion. Instead, my role throughout *Monster Diary* has been to *share* with you the extraordinary stories I uncovered in that three year span. If, after reading these words, you have come to accept the material as being valid, then that's fine. That being the case, you will now very likely find yourself looking at the enigmatic animals of planet Earth with new respect and, perhaps, even with new degrees of awe and trepidation. If, however, such tales outrage you, purely because they are not filled with heard-it-all-before data on Sasquatch DNA, scat, hair analysis, plaster-casts of giant, humanoid footprints, and audio recordings of ominous growls and grunts, then nothing I or the witnesses can ever say will likely change your mind about the nature of the phenomenon.

Monsters exist. They really do. And monster hunters have been faithfully patrolling dark forests, the shorelines of sprawling lakes and lochs, and the heart of ancient landscapes for decades in pursuit of them. But what have they got to show for all those decades of effort and dedication? Nothing conclusive at all, that's what. No body of Bigfoot, no definitive skin cells from a lake-monster, no werewolf fangs, no....well, you get what I'm saying.

As hard as it has tried, the community of cryptozoologists has failed to prove that unknown, or presumed extinct, flesh and blood animals are running around the woods, swimming in the waters, or flying in the skies of our world. There has to be a reason why this effort has been a complete, unrelenting failure. The most obvious explanation—for the skeptics, anyway—would be that the creatures don't exist in the first place. But they clearly *do* exist in some odd way.

Quite simply, monsters are not what most monster hunters assume them to be, or even want them to be. As long as the creature-seeking community continues to pursue that one pathway—the one that leads only to physical specimens, dead or alive—the chase is practically destined to always be a fruitless one, filled with tale after tale of the fisherman variety: the one that got away, the one that is *always* going to get away. Unless, of course, the field of cryptozoology wakes up and realizes that there needs to be a new approach to the subject.

But I have no intention of holding my breath.

Photo Gallery

From the wilds of Wales to the canals of England, stories abound of serpentine monsters roaming the British landscape and lurking in its deep waters. (Edward Topsell)

A Winona peak: the site of an extraordinary encounter with a giant winged beast. (Nick Redfern)

*(Right)
Tales of huge,
flying monsters
have been reported
in the vicinity
of Wisconsin's
Trempealeau
Mountain for
centuries. (Edward
Newman)*

*(Below)
A dead frog atop a
mini-Stonehenge:
occult sacrifice
in Nick Redfern's
yard? (Nick
Redfern)*

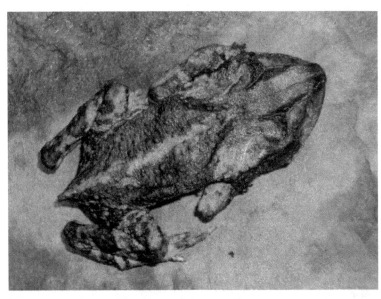

(Above) A creepy-looking stone head found at the location of a Texas-based werewolf encounter. (Nick Redfern)

(Below) The Cardiff Giant: a 19th Century hoax comes to life as a monster of the mind. (Unknown)

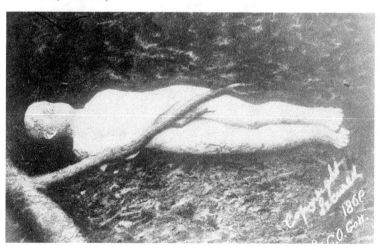

Giant Rock, California: home to contactees, space brothers, and ghostly camels. (Nick Redfern)

In late 2010, the legendary, glowing-eyed Owlman resurfaced—at Giant Rock. (Nick Redfern)

U. S. AIR FORCE

PROJECT RAND

RESEARCH MEMORANDUM

THE EXPLOITATION OF SUPERSTITIONS FOR
PURPOSES OF PSYCHOLOGICAL WARFARE (U)

Jean M. Hungerford

RM-365

ASTIA Document Number ATI 210637

14 April 1950

Assigned to _____

This is a working paper. It may be expanded, modified, or with-
drawn at any time. The views, conclusions, and recommendations
expressed herein do not necessarily reflect the official views or
policies of the United States Air Force.

The RAND *Corporation*
1700 MAIN ST. • SANTA MONICA • CALIFORNIA

34 pp

Was the notorious Flatwoods Monster of 1952 nothing less than a top secret creation of the Pentagon? (RAND)

George Edalji was accused of animal mutilations and occult rituals in early-20th century England. (Unknown)

PHOTO GALLERY   167

Devil's Gate Dam: Pasadena's most paranormal and monstrous place. (Nick Redfern)

MONSTER DIARY

Acknowledgments

I would like to offer my very sincere thanks to all of the following people:

Patrick Huyghe and Dennis Stacy of Anomalist Books, without whose longstanding dedication to the world of Fortean publishing you would not now be reading this book; Jill O'Brien, Joshua P. Warren, and Jenny Burrows, for discussing with me their experiences and thoughts on animals of the spectral type; Huw Fowler, whose testimony continues to fly the flag of the Beast of Bodalog, almost a quarter of a century after it first surfaced; John Weatherley and Gordon Moseley, for sharing their memories of giant eels; Chase Kloetzke, my partner in crime on the Oklahoma Bigfoot hunt of 2011; Neil and Jemma Arnold, for having the courage to reveal the details of their close encounter of the supernatural snake variety; Dr. Dan Holdsworth, for the drives and the jokes; Jon Downes and Corinna Downes, the finest of friends and the perfect couple; Richard Freeman for, well, for being Richard; Mark Petersen for his thoughts and observations on Bigfoot and the Mothman; great friend Greg Bishop, with whom hanging out is always a great and fun experience; Kristin Howard, for being willing to share her story of the Bigfoot of Angel Fire, New Mexico; Marlene Devorss and Mack Barlow, whose testimony demonstrates the Goat Man of Lake Worth, Texas, is not as dead as many assume it to be; Ken Gerhard, a fine mate and seeker of the strange; Raven Meindel, for her friendship and her dedicated work in the field of Forteana; Regan Lee, whose research and writing in the field of the contactee movement has proved to be illuminating in the extreme; each and every one of the SyFy Channel's *Ghost Hunters* crew; Real and Chance, with whom— just maybe— I caught sight of a Skinwalker one night in the summer of 2010; Fred Goodson and Jordan, for their tales of, and experiences with, California's ghostly camels; Jaclyn Schultz of Fox News, for inviting me to investigate the Chupacabras of Tecumseh, Oklahoma; Don Johnson, for his tales of the Taigheirm terror; Jonathan Crossland, a man who may very well have proved that George Edalji was not the villain many portrayed him to be; Mike Roberts, for organizing the Cryptid Fest gig; Bob Jessup for his diabolical tale of Devil's Gate Dam; Naomi and Richie West, for kindly sharing with me their information on the Owlman; and last of all, but most assuredly not least of all, my dad, Frank, without whose trusty Fiat, a significant body of material contained in this book would never have been secured!

I would also like to acknowledge the late Gabe Valdez, an all-round good guy, a major contributor to the controversies surrounding the alleged underground alien base at Dulce, New Mexico, as well as its attendant cattle mutilation mystery, and someone who displayed incredible generosity when Greg Bishop and I met with him for lunch in September 2009.

Sources

Chapter 1: *Creatures of the Spectral Kind*

1. *Mammoth: The Resurrection of an Ice Age Giant*, Richard Stone, Fourth Estate, 2005; *Twilight of the Mammoths*, Paul S. Martin, University of California Press, Berkeley, 2005

2. *Siberian Expedition: Wrangel Island*, http://www.amnh.org/exhibitions/expeditions/siberia/

3. *Extinct Elephant Still Alive?* Tabitca, http://cryptozoo-oscity.blogspot.com/2009/05/extinct-elephant-still-alive.html, May 19 2009

4. *Argus*, February 1888

5. *The Killing of the Mammoth*, Henry Tukeman, *McClure's Magazine*, October 1899

6. *In Search of the Last Mammoth*, Nick Redfern, *Darklore, Vol. 5*. Daily Grail Publishing, 2010

7. Ibid.

8. Ibid.

9. *Mammoth*, http://www.imdb.com/title/tt0487037/; *Primeval*, http://www.itv.com/primeval; *10,000 BC*, http://10000bcmovie.com

10. *Wrangell-St. Elias*, http://www.nps.gov/wrst/index.htm

11. Interview with Jill O'Brien, January 9, 2009

12. *Saber-toothed Cats*, http://exhibits.museum.state.il.us/exhibits/larson/smilodon.html

13. *Sabretooth*, http://www.imdb.com/title/tt0284445/

14. *Primeval*, http://www.itv.com/primeval

15. Interview with Jenny Burrows, January 23, 2009

16. *Man-Monkey: In Search of the British Bigfoot*, Nick Redfern, CFZ Press, 2007

17. *Sheldrake's Aldershot & Sandhurst Military Gazette*, December 8, 1878

18. *A British Bigfoot?* Mike Dash, http://blogs.forteana.org/node/65, February 11, 2009

19. *Cat-Flaps!* Andy Roberts, CFZ Press, 2007

20. *Pet Ghosts*, Joshua P. Warren, New Page Books, 2006; Interview with Joshua P. Warren, July 5, 2010

21. *PSI Spies*, Jim Marrs, New Page Books, 2007

Chapter 2: *Beware the Beast of Bodalog*

1. *Rhayader*, http://www.rhayader.co.uk/
2. *The Bodalog Monster*, Nick Redfern, *Lair of the Beasts*, http://www.mania.com/lair-beasts-bodalog-monster_article_122821.html, May 29, 2010; *A Water Vampire*, Karl Shuker, *Fate*, March 1990.
3. *Dragons: More Than a Myth?* Richard Freeman, CFZ Press, 2005.
4. *The Great Eel of Birmingham*, Nick Redfern, http://monsterusa.blogspot.com/2008/04/great-eel-of-birmingham.html, April 18, 2008
5. *Kelpie*, http://en.wikipedia.org/wiki/Kelpie
6. *Leviticus*, http://www.biblegateway.com/passage/?search=Leviticus+1&version=NIV
7. *The Folk-Lore of Herefordshire*, Ella Mary Leather, S.R. Publishers, 1970.
8. Interview with Huw Fowler, August 7, 2009.

Chapter 3: *The Great Eel Hunt*

1. *Man-Monkey: In Search of the British Bigfoot*, Nick Redfern, CFZ Press, 2007
2. Interview with Norman Dodd, September 7, 1995
3. *15-Foot Python Dead in Canal*, Steve Swingler, http://icbirmingham.icnetwork.co.uk/0100news/0100localnews/page.cfm?objectid=12562014&method=full&si, January 23, 2003; *Giant Eels - A Breaking Story*, Nick Redfern, http://monsterusa.blogspot.com/2007/04/giant-eels-breaking-story.html, April 6, 2007
4. Email from John Weatherley to Nick Redfern, April 5, 2007
5. Email from John Weatherley to Nick Redfern, April 9, 2007
6. Email from Gordon Moseley to Nick Redfern, March 22, 2009; Interview with Gordon Moseley, March 27, 2009
7. *What Happened to me at the 'Weird Weekend'?* Neil Arnold, http://forteanzoology.blogspot.com/2009/10/neil-arnold-what-happened-to-me-at.html, October 12, 2009

Chapter 4: *Winged Things of Wisconsin*

1. *The Mothman Prophecies*, John Keel, Tor, 2001;
   Alien Animals, Janet & Colin Bord, Stackpole Books, 1981;
   The Silver Bridge, Gray Barker, BookSurge Publishing, 2008;
   Mothman and Other Curious Encounters, Loren Coleman,
   Paraview, 2002
2. Ibid.
3. Ibid.
4. Ibid.
5. Ibid.
6. Ibid.
7. Ibid.
8. Ibid.
9. Ibid.
10. *Mothman and Other Curious Encounters*, Loren Coleman,
    Paraview, 2002
11. *Beyond Mothman: I-35W Blues*, Loren Coleman,
    http://www.cryptomundo.com/cryptozoo-news/i-35w-blues/,
    August 5, 2007
12. *The Owlman and Others*, Jonathan Downes, CFZ Press, 2006
13. *Three Men Seeking Monsters*, Nick Redfern, Paraview-Pocket
    Books, 2004
14. *The Brentford Griffin*, Andrew Collins, Earthquest Books,
    1985
15. *Sex Mad 'Ghost' Scares Nanzibaris*, Ally Saleh,
    http://news.bbc.co.uk/2/hi/africa/1446733.stm, July 19,
    2001;
    Three Men Seeking Monsters, Nick Redfern, Paraview-Pocket
    Books, 2004
16. *Mimic*, http://www.imdb.com/title/tt0119675/
17. *MonsterQuest*, http://www.history.com/shows/monsterquest
18. *The Beast of Bray Road and Hunting the American Werewolf
    Home Page*,
    http://beastofbrayroad.com
19. *Monsters of Wisconsin*, Linda S. Godfrey, Stackpole Books,
    2011
20. *Perrot State Park*, http://dnr.wi.gov/org/land/parks/specific/
    perrot/
21. *Jeepers Creepers*, http://www.imdb.com/title/tt0263488/

Chapter 5: *The Monsters of Angel Fire*

1. *Project Beta*, Greg Bishop, Paraview-Pocket Books, 2005
2. *Paying Respects*, Nick Redfern, http://nickspicoftheday. blogspot.com/2011/09/paying-respects.html, September 7, 2011
3. *The Angel Fire Monsters*, Nick Redfern, http:// nickspicoftheday.blogspot.com/2011/12/angel-fire-monsters. html, December 15, 2011
4. *Mysteries at Angel Fire*, Nick Redfern, http://aforteancalendar.blogspot.com/2009/07/mysteries-at-angel-fire.html, July 30, 2009
5. Emails from Kristin Howard to Nick Redfern, September 27 and 30, October 9 and 16, and November 7, 2009
6. *Monsters of Texas*, Ken Gerhard & Nick Redfern, CFZ Press, 2010
7. *The Lake Worth Monster*, Sallie Ann Clarke, self-published, 1969
8. *Fort Worth Nature Center and Refuge*, http://www. fwnaturecenter.org/
9. *Southern Fried Bigfoot*, http://southernfriedbigfoot.com
10. *Are you hunting for Cam the Man?* http://www.camtheman.net
11. *Skip Pullig Band*, http://www.skippullig.net
12. Interview with Mack Barlow, October 3, 2009
13. Interview with Marion Devorss, October 3, 2009

Chapter 6: *Sacrificed Frogs and Stone-Faced Werewolves*

1. *Contactees*, Nick Redfern, New Page Books, 2009
2. *The Mystical Contactee Encounters of Dana Howard: Parallels to Marian Apparitions?* Regan Lee, http://www.ufodigest.com/ news/1207/danahoward.html, December 20, 2007
3. *Venus is Speaking: Synchronicities, Contactees and Kitchens*, Regan Lee, http://reganlee.wordpress.com/2009/07/31/venus-is-speaking-synchronicities-contactees-and-kitchens/, July 31, 2009
4. Ibid.
5. *The Weirdness Continues...*, Nick Redfern, http:// contacteesbook.blogspot.com/2009/12/weirdness-continues. html, December 2, 2009
6. *Looking for Orthon*, Colin Bennett, Paraview Press, 2001
7. *Liber LXX, The Cross of a Frog*, http://hermetic.com/crowley/

libers/lib70.html
8. *Frogs in Popular Culture*, http://en.wikipedia.org/wiki/Frogs_ in_popular_culture
9. *Final Events*, Nick Redfern, Anomalist Books, 2010
10. *MILABS: Military Mind Cobtrol & Alien Abduction*, Helmutt Lammer & Marion Lammer, IllumiNet Press, 1999
11. Ibid.
12. *Aboard a Flying Saucer*, Truman Bethurm & Mary Kay Tennison, DeVorss & Co., 1954
13. Interview with Walter, August 20, 2006

Chapter 7: *The Curious Caper of the Cardiff Giant*

1. *Ghost Hunters*, http://www.syfy.com/ghosthunters/
2. *The Great Cardiff Giant*, http://www.lhup.edu/~dsimanek/ cardiff.htm;
The Cardiff Giant, http://www.museumofhoaxes.com/hoax/ archive/permalink/the_cardiff_giant;
Cardiff Giant, Cooperstown, New York, http://www. roadsideamerica.com/story/2172;
A Colossal Hoax: The Giant from Cardiff that Fooled America, Scott Tribble, Rowman & Littlefield Publishers, 2010

Chapter 8: *Shape-Shifters and Creepy Camels*

1. Raven Meindel, July 9, 2010
2. *Hunt for the Skinwalker*, Colm A. Kelleher & George Knapp, Paraview-Pocket Books, 2005
3. *Real and Chance: The Legend Hunters*, http://www.vh1.com/shows/real_and_chance...legend_ hunters/series.jhtml
4. *Contactees*, Nick Redfern, New Page Books, 2009
5. *The U.S. Camel Corps: An Army Experiment*, Odie B. Faulk, Oxford University Press, 1976;
Camels to California, Harlan D. Fowler, Stanford University Press, Stanford, 1950;
Camels for Uncle Sam, Diane Yancey, Hendrick-Long Publishing Co., 1995
6. *Contactees*, Nick Redfern, New Page Books, 2009

Chapter 9: *Chasing the Chupacabras*

1. *Memoirs of a Monster Hunter*, Nick Redfern, New Page Books, 2007
2. Ibid.
3. Ibid.
4. *Paranatural*, http://natgeotv.com/asia/paranatural
5. *Monsters of Texas*, Ken Gerhard & Nick Redfern, CFZ Press, 2010
6. Ibid.
7. Ibid.
8. Ibid.
9. *Chupacabra Sighting in Oklahoma*, http://www.okcfox.com/newsroom/special_reports/videos/vid_191.shtml

Chapter 10: *The Rise of the Owlman*

1. *Owl on a Cold Winter's Night*, Mike Clelland, http://hiddenexperience.blogspot.com/2010/12/owl-on-cold-winters-night.html, December 20, 2010
2. *Another Strange Case of Synchronicity*, Naomi West, http://westruth.blogspot.com/2010/12/another-strange-case-of-synchronicity.html, December 23, 2010
3. Ibid.
4. *Odor of the Owl*, Regan Lee, http://animalforteana.blogspot.com/2010/12/odor-of-owl.html, December 27, 2010
5. Email from Davy Allen, December 28, 2010
6. Email from Naomi West, December 27, 2011
7. Email from Naomi West, December 28, 2011

Chapter 11: *The Taigheirm Terror*

1. Parliamentary copyright material from Commons Hansard, February 2, 1998, is reproduced with the permission of the Controller of Her Majesty's Stationery Office, in behalf of the British Government's Parliament
2. *Opening the Government's X-Archive*, Nick Redfern, *Daily Express*, September 12, 2006
3. Ibid.
4. Ibid.
5. Interview with Eileen Allen, June 4, 2009

6. Interviews with Bob Parker, January 8 and 12, 2001
7. Interview with Sally Ward, May 29, 2009
8. *The Owlman and Others*, Jonathan Downes, CFZ Press, 2006
9. Ibid.
10. Ibid.
11. *Mystery Big Cats*, Merrily Harpur, Heart of Albion Press, 2006
12. Ibid.
13. *The History of the Prince, the Lord's Marcher, and the Ancient Nobility of Powys Fadog and the Ancient Lords of Arwystli, Cedewen, and Meirionydd*, J.Y.W. Lloyd, T. Richards Press, 1881
14. Ibid.
15. Ibid.
16. Ibid.
17. Ibid.
18. *The Tiger in the House*, Carl Van Vechten, NYRB Classics, 2007
19. *Mystery Big Cats*, Merrily Harpur, Heart of Albion Press, 2006
20. *The Mystery Animals of the British Isles: The Western Isles*, Glen Vaudrey, 2009

Chapter 12: *Slaughter in Dallas*

1. *Here, Puss! Puss! Puss!*, *Chase Post*, January 2000;
   Chase Beast's Getting Bolder, *Chase Post*, March 2, 2000
2. Ibid.
3. Ibid.
4. *Lair of the Beasts: Alligators on the Rampage*, Nick Redfern, http://www.mania.com/lair-beasts-alligators-rampage_ article_121013.html, March 5, 2010;
   Lair of the Beasts: Exotic Animals Increasing, Nick Redfern, http://www.mania.com/lair-beasts-exotic-animals-increasing_ article_130601.html, July 23, 2011
5. *Cause of Cat Mutilation Undetermined*, http://lakewood.advocatemag.com/2009/07/cause-of-cat-mutilation-undetermined/, July 22, 2009
6. *Cats Found Mutilated, Cut in Half, Dallas, TX (US)*, http://pet-abuse.com/cases/15756/TX/US/August 26, 2009
7. *Mutilated Cats Discovered in Dallas Neighborhood*, Ken Kalthoff, http://www.nbcdfw.com/news/local/Mutilated-Cats-Discovered-in-Dallas-Neighborhood-54858612.html, August

26, 2009

8. *Mutilated Cat Found Dead in Wilshire Heights Near Skillman*, Nancy Visser, http://eastdallasblog.dallasnews.com/archives/2011/04/mutilated-cat-found-dead-in-wi.html, April 14, 2011

9. *Secrets of the Tomb: Skull and Bones, the Ivy League, and the Hidden Paths of Power*, Alexandra Robbins, Back Bay Books, 2003

10. *Crime Blog: Police say 'tigers' spotted in downtown Dallas were probably Bobcats*, Matt Peterson, http://www.dallasnews.com/news/community-news/dallas/headlines/20100720-crime-blog-police-say-tigers_spotted-in-downtown-dallas-were-probably-bobcats.ece, July 20, 2010

11. *Supernatural Sacrifice*, Donald Johnson, publication pending

Chapter 13: *Monsters and the Government*

1. *The Braxton County Monster*, Frank Feschino, Quarrier Press, 2004

2. *The Flatwoods Monster*, Kevin Randle, *A Different Perspective*, http://kevinrandle.blogspot.com/2011/03/flatwoods-monster.html, March 23, 2011

3. *The Exploitation of Superstitions for Purposes of Psychological Warfare*, Jean M. Hungerford, RAND, April 14, 1950

4. *Magic: Top Secret*, Jasper Maskelyne, S. Paul Publishers, 1949

5. Ibid.

6. Interview with Rich Reynolds, June 23, 2009

7. *Unearthly Batman Terrifies Watchers, Houston Chronicle*, June 19, 1953

8. *Monsters of Texas*, Ken Gerhard & Nick Redfern, CFZ Press, 2010

9. Email, September 14, 2010

10. *Body Snatchers in the Desert*, Nick Redfern, Paraview-Pocket Books, 2005

11. *Bacteriological Warfare in the United States, 1941-1950*, Federal Bureau of Investigation, 1951

Chapter 14: *Ripping Yarns*

1. *Pelsall History Centre*, Steve Dent, http://www.pelsall-history.co.uk/, 2011;
    Pelsall Online, http://www.crutchleyhistory.co.uk/pelsall/

2. Ibid.
3. *Great Wyrley*, http://en.wikipedia.org/wiki/Great_Wyrley
4. *Conan Doyle and the Parson's Son: The George Edalji Case*, Gordon Weaver, Vanguard Press, 2006;
   The Case of Mr. George Edalji, Sir Arthur Conan Doyle, Classic Books, 2000;
   Arthur & George, Julian Barnes, Vintage, 2007;
   The Story of Mr. George Edalji, Sir Arthur Conan Doyle, introduction by Richard & Molly Whittington-Egan, Grey House Books, 1985;
   The George Edalji Case, Birmingham City Council, http://www.birmingham.gov.uk/edalji
5. Interview with Jonathan Crossland, March 14, 2011
6. *Conan Doyle and the Parson's Son: The George Edalji Case*, Gordon Weaver, Vanguard Press, 2006;
   The Case of Mr. George Edalji, Sir Arthur Conan Doyle, Classic Books, 2000;
   Arthur & George, Julian Barnes, Vintage, 2007;
   The Story of Mr. George Edalji, Sir Arthur Conan Doyle, introduction by Richard & Molly Whittington-Egan, Grey House Books, 1985;
   The George Edalji Case, Birmingham City Council, http://www.birmingham.gov.uk/edalji
7. Ibid.
8. *The Mystery Animals of the British Isles: Staffordshire*, Nick Redfern CFZ Press, 2012
9. *Conan Doyle and the Parson's Son: The George Edalji Case*, Gordon Weaver, Vanguard Press, 2006;
   The Case of Mr. George Edalji, Sir Arthur Conan Doyle, Classic Books, 2000;
   Arthur & George, Julian Barnes, Vintage, 2007;
   The Story of Mr. George Edalji, Sir Arthur Conan Doyle, introduction by Richard & Molly Whittington-Egan, Grey House Books, 1985;
   The George Edalji Case, Birmingham City Council, http://www.birmingham.gov.uk/edalji
10. *There's something in the Woods*, Nick Redfern, Anomalist Books, 2008
11. *The Mystery Animals of the British Isles: Staffordshire*, Nick Redfern CFZ Press, 2012
12. Ibid.
13. Ibid.

14. Ibid.
15. Ibid.
16. *Conan Doyle and the Parson's Son: The George Edalji Case*, Gordon Weaver, Vanguard Press, 2006;
    The Case of Mr. George Edalji, Sir Arthur Conan Doyle, Classic Books, 2000;
    Arthur & George, Julian Barnes, Vintage, 2007;
    The Story of Mr. George Edalji, Sir Arthur Conan Doyle, introduction by Richard & Molly Whittington-Egan, Grey House Books, 1985;
    The George Edalji Case, Birmingham City Council, http://www.birmingham.gov.uk/edalji
17. Interview with Jonathan Crossland, March 14, 2011
18. *The Case of the Cannock Croc*, Mark P. Martin, http://www.cfz.org.uk/expeditions/03croc/croc-mm-account.htm;
    Crocodile Hunting in the Midlands, Jonathan Downes, http://www.cfz.org.uk/expeditions/03croc/crocindex.htm
19. *Water-Beasts of the Midlands – A New Theory*, Nick Redfern, July 15, 2010, http://monsterusa.blogspot.com/2010/07/water-beasts-of-midlands-new-theory.html
20. Interview with Terry Baxter, July 8, 2010
21. *Hobgoblin at Hobbs Point*, Loren Coleman, http://www.cryptomundo.com/cryptozoo-news/hobbs-hob/, August 10, 2008

Chapter 15: *Dead Heads, Demons, and a Damned Dam*

1. *Cryptid Fest*, http://www.cryptidfest.com/
2. *Fox on the Town: Hunt for Bigfoot*, Stephanie Hastings, http://www.kxii.com/fox/headlines/129929858.html, September 16, 2011
3. *E.P.I.C Voyages*, http://epicvoyagers.com
4. *Bigfoot Wood Knocking? Or...*, Craig Woolheater, http://www.cryptomundo.com/bigfoot-report/bigfoot-wood-knocking-or/, June 10, 2011
5. Email from Neil Arnold to Nick Redfern, September 30, 2011
6. Email from Nick Redfern to Neil Arnold, October 4, 2011
7. Email from Neil Arnold to Nick Redfern, October 5, 2011
8. *Head-Hunting*, Nick Redfern, http://nickspicoftheday.blogspot.com/2011/09/head-hunting.html, September 27,

2011

9. *Chaos!* Nick Redfern, http://nickspicoftheday.blogspot. com/2011/10/chaos.html, October 18, 2011

10. *Final Events*, Nick Redfern, Anomalist Books, 2010

11. Interview with Bob Jessup, January 30, 2011

12. *Devil's Gate: A Portal to Hell?* http://laghostpatrol. com/2011/05/devils-gate/, May 18, 2011;
Mack Ray Edwards, http://en.wikipedia.org/wiki/Mack_Ray_ Edwards
Strange Disappearances at the Cursed Devil's Gate Reservoir, http://www.weirdus.com/states/california/unexplained_ phenomena /devils_gate_reservoir/index.php

Index

About Nick Redfern

Nick Redfern works full-time as an author, lecturer and journalist. He focuses upon a wide range of unsolved mysteries, including Bigfoot, UFOs, the Loch Ness Monster, alien encounters, and government conspiracies. He writes for *UFO Magazine; Mysterious Universe; Fate;* and *Fortean Times.* His many previous books include *Final Events; On the Trail of the Saucer Spies; There's something in the Woods;* and *Science Fiction Secrets.* Nick has appeared on numerous television shows, including Fox News; VH1's *Legend Hunters;* the BBC's *Out of this World;* History Channel's *America's Book of Secrets, Ancient Aliens, MonsterQuest* and *UFO Hunters;* National Geographic Channel's *The Truth About UFOs* and *Paranatural;* and SyFy Channel's *Proof Positive.* Nick Redfern can be contacted at http://nickredfernfortean.blogspot.com.

9 781933 665962

CPSIA information can be obtained
at www.ICGtesting.com
Printed in the USA
FSHW020648100420
69036FS